D0881110

# Richard Wagner and the Modern British Novel

ALSO BY John Louis DiGaetani:

*Penetrating Wagner's Ring: An Anthology* (Editor)

# Richard Wagner and the Modern British Novel

*John Louis DiGaetani*

Rutherford • Madison • Teaneck
Fairleigh Dickinson University Press
London: Associated University Presses

Associated University Presses, Inc.
Cranbury, New Jersey 08512

Associated University Presses
Magdalen House
136-148 Tooley Street
London SE1 2TT, England

**Library of Congress Cataloging in Publication Data**
DiGaetani, John Louis, 1943-
Richard Wagner and the modern British novel.

Bibliography: p.
Includes index.
1. English fiction—20th century—History and criticism. 2. Wagner, Richard, 1813-1883—Influence. 3. Myth in literature.
PR888.W34D5 823'.03 76-744
ISBN 0-8386-1955-X



PRINTED IN THE UNITED STATES OF AMERICA

*For Jane*

# CONTENTS

# Acknowledgments

I wish to thank the following publishers for having given me permission to quote from published works:

Edward Arnold Publishers, for permission to quote from E. M. Forster, *Aspects of the Novel*, 1954.

Harcourt Brace Jovanovich, Inc., for permission to quote from E. M. Forster, *Aspects of the Novel*, 1954; Quentin Bell, *Virginia Woolf: A Biography*, 1972; Virginia Woolf, *The Voyage Out*, 1949, and Virginia Woolf, *The Years*, 1965.

The Hogarth Press and the author's literary estate, for permission to quote from Virginia Woolf, *The Voyage Out*, 1948, and Virginia Woolf, *The Years*, 1965.

The Hogarth Press and the author, for permission to quote from Quentin Bell, *Virginia Woolf: A Biography*, 1972.

The Viking Press, Inc., for permission to quote from *Letters of James Joyce*, Vol. II, edited by Richard Ellmann. Copyright © 1966 by F. Lionel Munro. All Rights Reserved. Reprinted by permission of the Viking Press, Inc.

I also wish to record my gratitude to several people who helped my research, edited my manuscript, or personally encouraged me with this book. In Madison, Paul Wiley, Walter Rideout, Robert Mitchell, Michael Bemis, and Barbara Guenther. In New Orleans, Robert Bourdette, Earl Harbert, Marcus Smith, Elizabeth Ashen, and Evelyn Chandler. In New Jersey, Mathilde Finch. In Atlanta, Gil Adkins. In Chicago, my parents. Finally, my wife.

# Acknowledgments

# Introduction

Walter Pater became famous in the 1890s for his statement that "all art constantly aspires towards the condition of music."[1] But music and literature are natural enemies. The specificity of words is, of its essence, antagonistic to the abstraction of music. When words become too abstract, the effect is often vague, confusing, and finally boring—Kant, Santayana, and Carlyle immediately come to mind as obvious examples. When music becomes too specific, the resultant bird calls and shepherd pipes can easily sound silly and obvious, as in some of Strauss's less successful tone poems or Respighi's superficial descriptions of Italian scenery written, one suspects, for the naive tourist and Il Duce. But through drama, literature and music can come together in what is often called the bastard art form, opera. Some would argue, of course, that what is generally produced is the pathetic, boring combination of dreary doggerel with a silly tune. Too often in opera, the action stops for the tenors and sopranos to show off their voices. The rhythm of "*stride la vampa*" is great fun in *Il Trovatore*, but has little to do with the atmosphere of the drama. If the drama stops, some would say that this doesn't really matter if the tune is worth the delay; but the great theoreticians of opera, like Count Bardi, Gluck, and Wagner, have always been very uncomfortable with these musical delays and theorized about the ideal dramatic combination of music and poetry that would result in great opera.

Admittedly, for most of its history opera has not come close to this ideal and for this reason it has rarely attracted intellectuals or writers. The good tune was for the lazy aristocrat or the general public, not the solitary writer or thinker. But interestingly, the five greatest English novelists of this century became very much interested in opera. That figures of the enormous literary stature of Joseph Conrad, D. H. Lawrence, E. M. Forster, Virginia Woolf, and James Joyce should become fascinated by opera, of all art forms, is a tribute to the composer they were most interested in, Richard Wagner. As William Blissett has said: "Anyone concerned with Wagnerism as a cultural phenomenon—arguably the greatest single fact to be reckoned with in the arts during the past century—will have noticed the large number of novels that relate themselves to Wagner's life or works in their fables, that describe their persons as undergoing an experience of Wagner's music, or that attempt to capture in literature by structure or technique the effects of Wagnerian music-drama."[2]

This study shows how, why, and where these writers became interested in the operas of the German composer, and how the experience affected their fiction. When one is really serious, we all know, one does not sing. Why, then, were these five major novelists interested in the operas of an anti-Semitic, egotistical, German dwarf? What was it about these artists and the period in which they developed that attracted them to the composer? Exactly how was their fiction altered by the confrontation?

These five novelists reached intellectual maturity during the Edwardian period, when Wagner's operas were an important part of the intellectual climate. As a result, Wagnerian themes and allusions occurred often in the English fiction of the period, but these five writers used Wagnerian patterns in a peculiarly modern way, which will be defined precisely in the next five chapters. By *Wagnerian patterns* I mean allusions, themes, images, and symbols that can be connected with Wagner's operas. I begin my discussion of these writers' fiction with "Wagnerian allusions," specific allusions to the operas in the novels and short stories of the particular author. For example, Rachel Vinrace in Mrs. Woolf's *The Voyage Out* often plays Wagner on the piano and Freya in

Conrad's "Freya of the Seven Isles" also plays Wagner: these constitute allusions. Also, when Dixon whistles the forest-bird motif in Joyce's *A Portrait of the Artist as a Young Man*, we know that he is referring to *Siegfried*. Early in Lawrence's *Women in Love* Gerald Crich is called "a Nibelung," which connects with the Wagnerian operas based on that German myth. Conrad's "The Lagoon" employs a Wagnerian theme by portraying a *Tristan*-like love and death. Finally, Wagnerian images and symbols occur in these writers' fiction. By the Edwardian period a body of images and symbols had come into English fiction and their most direct source was Wagnerian opera. For example, the purifying fire at the end of Conrad's *Victory* is dependent in part upon Wagner's immolation scene at the end of *Götterdämmerung*. The extensive use of moonlight for Siegmund and Helena's love in Lawrence's *The Trespasser* parallels the light imagery for Siegmund and Sieglinde in *Die Walküre*. The rainbow bridge in Forster's *Howards End* is an allusion to the famous rainbow bridge at the end of *Rheingold*. Such a body of allusions, themes, images, and symbols constitutes what I have called Wagnerian patterns.

Each chapter looks at one of these five authors, beginning with an examination of his correspondence and essays for indications of the extent of his knowledge of Wagner and his operas. Once the particular author's awareness and appreciation of Wagner have been established through these sources, I discuss in chronological order the short stories and novels of that author that significantly employ Wagnerian patterns, showing exactly where the patterns occur and then investigating their purpose. Finally, each chapter ends with a summary of Wagner's influence upon the author under discussion. We shall see, by the conclusion, that Wagner's music-dramas exercised a subtle but profound effect upon these writers, most often by providing examples of the uses of myth for artistic purposes. *Myth* is a difficult term to define exactly, but for present purposes it is the use of ancient folk stories to explore metaphysical realities like the meaning of life, love, and death, and to chronicle the adventures of a folk hero.

Wagner was essentially a mythic artist. After his first three pieces of juvenilia, *Die Feen, Das Liebesverbot,* and *Rienzi*, he found in old Nordic myths and medieval legends the most congenial subjects for his operas. All his subsequent works, from *Der Fliegende Holländer* onwards, dramatize mythic stories like the Flying Dutchman, the legend of Tristan and Isolde, and the *Nibelungenlied*. Wagnerian myths became highly fashionable in Edwardian fiction, but Conrad, Lawrence, Woolf, and Joyce were distinctive in their uses of Wagnerian mythic patterns and some of them continued to use them even after World War I. For Forster, on the other hand, Wagnerian opera provided a means of structuring his novels to give them what he liked to call rhythm.

By the time Wagner died in Venice in 1883 his works were not in the standard repertory of any English opera house.[3] In an effort to raise funds for Bayreuth, Wagner himself went to London in the spring of 1877 and conducted a series of eight concerts. Although they failed to make much money for Bayreuth, they were critically successful and gained much attention among the artistic avant-garde. While Wagner was in London he met George Eliot, her husband George Lewes, and Robert Browning.[4] One of the first results of this attraction between intellectuals and artists and Wagner's operas was the appearance in 1881 of the first book on Wagner in English, Francis Hueffer's *Richard Wagner*. Hueffer, Ford Madox Ford's father, left his native Germany but remained a Wagnerian all his life and usually summered in Bayreuth. In addition to writing the pioneering book on the composer in English, he started a periodical entitled, appropriately, *Die Meister*. The journal was popular and served to further the cause of Wagner's music. In May of 1882 Angelo Neumann staged the entire *Ring* in London, and it was a popular success there. Even English royalty helped the Wagnerian cause, as recorded by Ernest Newman: "Neumann was very successful with this first production of the *Ring* in London. Thanks to an introduction from the German Crown Prince he managed to get the Prince of Wales (afterwards King Edward VII) to attend no fewer than eleven of the performances. The Prince had been so charmed by the swimming

Rhine Maidens that at one performance of the *Rhinegold* he went behind the scenes and expressed a desire to see the apparatus at work; but when he discovered that the occupant of the car was not to be the pretty young Augusta Kraus but one of the male stage hands he turned away with an impatient 'What the devil!' "[5] With the Prince of Wales' help, then, by 1882 London had seen onstage all the standard Wagnerian operas except for *Parsifal*.[6] With performances available in London and advocates like Francis Hueffer, the operas were becoming popular in England by the end of the 1800s.

The 90s became increasingly Wagnerian in their musical taste and this is reflected by many of the arts in England, but it was also a period of increasing critical awareness of the German composer. In 1898 Shaw wrote *The Perfect Wagnerite*, which summarized the complicated plot of the *Ring* and provided a Fabian socialist interpretation that is still generally sound. Shaw saw the *Ring* as a parable about the corrupting power of money, which causes the loss of both love and life for most of the people who desire it. Most critics since have used this basic interpretation, although changing some of its elements and eliminating most of Shaw's socialist doctrines.[7] *The Perfect Wagnerite* was very popular at the time and quickly went through many editions. In 1899 Ernest Newman's first book on Wagner appeared, *A Study of Wagner*, the first serious attempt in English to study the composer's musical techniques, dramatic methods, and aesthetic theories. Also in the 90s William Ashton Ellis was working on his eight-volume translation of Wagner's complete prose works, which appeared from 1895 to 1899. Within the next ten years Ellis would also translate Wagner's correspondence to his first wife, Minna Planer, and his most famous lover, Mathilde Wesendonck. Francis Hueffer's excellent two-volume translation of the correspondence of Wagner and Liszt was printed in 1897. In 1900 Jessie Weston's *The Legends of the Wagner Drama* appeared and was the first anthropological investigation of Wagner's literary and mythic sources. With critics and translators like Hueffer, Shaw, Newman, Ellis, and Weston, it is no wonder that Englishmen became increasingly aware of Wagnerian opera. During the 90s Covent Garden staged even more of Wagner's operas, which resulted in more popular awareness and appreciation of him. By 1899 *Lohengrin* had received one hundred performances at Covent Garden.[8]

Another major source of the Wagnerian influence on English culture at the end of the nineteenth century was the extensive Wagnerism of the intellectual and artistic trends coming from the Continent. Wagnerism, or the cult of Wagner, which included an adulation of his operas and his many essays on various subjects like race and the purpose of art, came from the Continent. But more important, many French writers who soon became famous in England were very fond of Wagner's operas and their work employed Wagnerian themes and methods. Villiers, Baudelaire, Verlaine, Zola, Proust, Valéry, Colette, Mallarmé, and Gautier all loved Wagnerian opera and their work reflects it.[9] Some of these writers praised the operas' librettos even more than the music. Also, some of these writers were publishing their work in Edouard Dujardin's *La Revue Wagnerienne*. Many of them became famous in England in the 90s, and through them Wagnerian elements were transmitted to English writers. Aesthetes and decadents like Wilde, Symons, and Beardsley exulted in the glories of French Symbolist poetry and made it fashionable in London in the 90s. Wagner has long been recognized as the father of French Symbolist poetry. Wilde, Beardsley, and Symons were especially influenced by French taste and shared its appreciation of Wagner. Beardsley did a series of lithographs on *Tannhäuser* to accompany his Wagnerian novelette, *Under the Hill*. Oscar Wilde's Dorian Gray was also fascinated with Wagnerian opera, as was Wilde himself. At one point in the novel Gray is described "listening in rapt pleasure to *Tannhäuser*, and seeing in the prelude to that great work of art a presentation of the tragedy of his own soul."[10] The conflict between the Venusberg music and the Pilgrim's Chorus in the prelude of the opera parallels Dorian Gray's own predicament and the allusion helps Wilde to portray it.

*Tannhäuser*-like conflict of sacred and profane love in the lives of the famous medieval lovers. But there, according to Brown, Moore experimented with the Wagnerian monologue as a prose form. Brown reports that Moore's later prose style, a flowing form of interior monologue, was based on Wagnerian monologues and was unified through the leitmotif.[13] The interior monologues in *Héloïse and Abélard* exemplify this more subtle use of Wagner's operas. The resultant effect, says Brown, is characterized by "the sense of *flow*, the essential trait of Moore's style in his last novels."[14] But the flow, says Brown, is governed by leitmotifs. This technique will be used much more subtly and effectively in the novels of E. M. Forster.

As the son of the famous Wagnerite Francis Hueffer, Ford Madox Ford inevitably absorbed a deep knowledge of the composer from his father. Ford's first novel, *The Shifting of the Fire* (1892), indicates an awareness of the composer with several Wagnerian allusions. According to Paul L. Wiley, the novel's repeated references to *Tristan und Isolde* help Ford to dramatize sexual passion in several of the characters,[15] while *The Nature of a Crime* (1924) also indicates a Wagnerian influence. Though the novel was written in collaboration with Joseph Conrad, Ford wrote most of it. Wiley says that the novel was "conceived in Edwardian times and in knowledge of Dostoevski. In this tale the narrator, writing to the married woman whom he has loved secretly, divulges his own motives while analyzing *Tristan*."[16] In this novel too, then, Ford uses Wagner to dramatize his characters' sexuality.

Arnold Bennett was also very fond of Wagner's operas, for his journal, which contains many references to them, recounts that he often went to hear Wagnerian performances. On February 13, 1897, he wrote: "At the opening bars of *The Flying Dutchman* I felt those strange tickling sensations in the back which are the physical signs of aesthetic emotion."[17] Toward the end of the journal, on May 31, 1925, Bennett concludes: "The power and beauty of Wagner are staggering."[18] Bennett's fondness for Wagner bore fruit in his novels. *Sacred and Profane Love* (1905),

Later, from Italy, came the Wagnerian novels of Gabriele D'Annunzio; there was even a legend that he had been one of Wagner's pallbearers in Venice. *Il Trionfo della Morte* (1896) and *Il Fuoco* (1898) were steeped in Wagnerian themes and symbols, especially from *Tristan und Isolde*.[11] These novels were immediately translated into English and became quite popular. From Germany came the Wagnerian fiction of Thomas Mann, whose "Tristan" (1902), "The Blood of the Walsungs" (1905), and *Death in Venice* (1911) all drew heavily on Wagnerian patterns. Nietzsche was first translated in the 90s and his strong opinions on the composer were discussed and written about in England.

Toward the end of the Decadent period the Wagner-inspired novel became popular in England. George Moore was most prominent in this genre. Throughout his life Moore went to Wagnerian performances, and many of his personal friends were also Wagnerites. Among them was Edouard Dujardin, the founder of *La Revue Wagnerienne*, who became associated with James Joyce in Paris in the 20s. Moore's *Evelyn Innes* (1898), which recounts the life of a Wagnerian soprano, indicates a detailed knowledge of the operas and their production. Malcolm Brown reports that Moore consulted several experts to insure the accuracy of the novel's musical background.[12] *Evelyn Innes*'s sequel, *Sister Teresa* (1901), begins with Evelyn's renunciation of her life as famous singer and mistress of Ulick Dean. She decides to join a convent, and the novel portrays her life there. Tannhäuser's conflict between sacred and sexual love is also basic to this novel, for his waverings between the religious love of Elizabeth and the passionate love of Venus is analogous to Evelyn's vacillation between the life of the opera singer and the nun's vocation. Both these novels use Wagnerian themes and allusions extensively to illustrate Evelyn's singing career and the conflicts in her personality. In both these novels Moore uses Wagnerian allusions for realistic characterization of women, but not to portray any mythic dimension in them or in the novels themselves. But in *Héloïse and Abélard* (1921) Moore uses Wagner in a different way. The novel also dramatizes a louder, speaking in an incomprehensible voice around the dumb darkness of that human sorrow. Arsat's eyes wandered slowly, then stared at the rising sun . . . 'I shall not eat or sleep in this house; but I must first see my road. Now I can see nothing—see nothing! There is no light and no peace in the world; but there is death—death for many' " (p. 203). The word *nothing* is dramatically effective in this passage—Conrad will use this word even more forcefully at the end of *Victory*. Arsat identifies his love with darkness, but the newly risen sun shines upon her corpse. In this truthful sunshine Arsat experiences the painful reality of death, yet he yearns for that glorious albeit illusory world of their love, which unfortunately is no more. The final lines of the story indicate Arsat's preference: "Before the sampan passed out of the lagoon into the creek he lifted his eyes. Arsat had not moved. He stood lonely in the searching sunshine; and he looked beyond the great light of a cloudless day into the darkness of a world of illusions" (p. 204). His love lived in a world of darkness and illusions, and his grief makes him desire it still. The unrealistic quality of the situation and the musical quality of the prose suggest opera—specifically *Tristan und Isolde*.

But the plight of Conrad's Malay Tristan and Isolde is made more painful by the presence of the white man. He does sympathize with the lovers, but with the condescension of a white man looking upon the quaint, darker races. Conrad explains the man's real position very early in the story: "He liked the man who knew how to keep faith in council and how to fight without fear by the side of his white friend. He liked him—not so much perhaps as a man likes his favorite dog—but still he liked him" (p. 191). This patronizing attitude provides a cynical background for the love and death in the story. The Wagnerian elements help to create a highly artificial and operatic world of metaphysical realities around the lovers; but Conrad includes the white man's condescension as well, for contrast and to anchor the story to a less philosophical and abstract base. He will often use narrators and Wagnerian patterns this way in the future.

as the very title suggests, refers repeatedly to Wagner's *Tannhäuser*. The novel describes the loving dedication of Carlotta and her efforts to save an alcoholic, ruined pianist and enable him to perform once again. The Wagnerian allusions help to communicate the novel's theme of sexual and religious love in conflict and to illustrate the essentially religious nature of Carlotta's love for the pianist.

By the 20s, however, such obvious uses of Wagnerian opera appeared dated and part of the pre-World War I intellectual climate. Bennett's novels declined in popularity, as did Ford's and Moore's, and all were criticized by the younger generation of writers. Virginia Woolf's "Mr. Bennett and Mrs. Brown" (1924) posits an essential failure of characterization in Bennett's novels. Joyce's fiction after World War I also tends to parody Wagner and his operas more frequently. However, a typically modern use of Wagner appeared in T. S. Eliot's *The Waste Land* (1922). The poem contains four quotations from the operas—two from *Tristan und Isolde* (ll. 31-35 and line 42) and two from *Götterdämmerung* (ll. 277-78 and lines 289-90)—as well as a line from Verlaine's sonnet on *Parsifal* (l. 202). The lines from *Tristan* are part of the poem's theme of neurotic, sterile, and unhappy love, and these references to Wagner's mythic opera of fated love add a mythic element to Eliot's poem. The quotations from *Götterdämmerung* add to the mythic quality of the poem by its inclusion of aspects of Wagner's vision of the death of a corrupted civilization. This use of Wagner is similar to the more modern ways that Conrad, Lawrence, Woolf, and Joyce employ Wagnerian patterns.

As we have seen, many elements and people helped to popularize Wagnerian opera in England. Beardsley, Wilde, Moore, Ford, and Bennett used Wagner's operas for purposes as varied as characterization, theme, and structure. But these are all minor novelists, and their uses of Wagner were often painfully unsubtle and obvious. Henry James once said that "the flower of art blooms only where the soil is deep, that it takes a great deal of history to produce a little literature."[19] In the next five chapters we shall investigate the peculiarly modern, subtle uses of Wagnerian patterns that occurred in the literature of Conrad, Lawrence, Forster, Woolf, and Joyce. Significantly, all five of these great novelists developed most of their intellectual and artistic roots during the Edwardian period, the time when Wagner was most popular. We shall see how each of these writers used Wagnerian patterns to create their own modern versions of a fiction that combined music with words. And, as we shall see, the results were not bastardization but hybridization.

## Notes

1. Walter Pater, "The School of Giorgione," *The Renaissance* (New York, n.d.), p.111.
2. William Blissett, "Wagnerian Fiction in English," *Criticism* 5 (Summer 1963): p. 239.
3. Alfred Loewenberg, *Annals of Opera: 1597-1940* (Cambridge, 1943), pp. 419, 432, 499, 515, 545, and 567.
4. Robert W. Gutman, *Richard Wagner: The Man, His Mind, and His Music* (New York, 1968), pp. 429-31.
5. Ernest Newman, *The Life of Richard Wagner* (New York, 1946), 4:673.
6. Loewenberg, pp. 419, 432, 451, 499, 515, 545, and 567. Loewenberg gives the following first-performance dates for London: *Der Fliegende Holländer*, 1870; *Tannhäuser*, 1876; *Lohengrin*, 1875; *Tristan und Isolde*, 1882; *Die Meistersinger*, 1882; the *Ring*, 1882; *Parsifal*, 1884 (concert version; first staged in London in 1914).
7. Ernest Newman's *The Wagner Operas*, Robert Donington's *Wagner's "Ring" and Its Symbols*, and Lawrence Gilman's *Wagner's Operas* all use Shaw's interpretation of the *Ring* as a conflict of love and money.
8. Loewenberg, p. 451.
9. Bryan Magee, *Aspects of Wagner* (New York, 1968), pp. 89-91.
10. Oscar Wilde, *The Picture of Dorian Gray* (London, 1895), p. 201.
11. Eurialo De Michelis, *Tutto D'Annunzio* (Milan, 1960), pp. 64, 143-49, 205-8.
12. Malcolm Brown, *George Moore: A Reconsideration* (Seattle, Wash., 1955), pp. 141-42.
13. Ibid., pp. 182-83.
14. Ibid., p. 184.
15. Paul L. Wiley, *Novelist of Three Worlds: Ford Madox Ford* (Syracuse, N.Y., 1962), p. 137.
16. Ibid., pp. 137-38.
17. Arnold Bennett, *The Journal of Arnold Bennett* (New York, 1933), pp. 34-35.
18. Ibid., p. 827.
19. Henry James, *Hawthorne* (New York, 1879), p. 3.

# Richard Wagner and the Modern British Novel

# 1
# "The Magic Suggestiveness of Music": Richard Wagner and Joseph Conrad

Joseph Conrad was not a Wagnerian in any strict sense of the word. He saw many of Wagner's operas but still, according to John Galsworthy, preferred Bizet.[1] Yet I contend and will attempt to prove in this chapter that Richard Wagner's operas had a subtle and profound influence upon Conrad's fiction. Was this simply a matter of unconscious absorption of the intellectual milieu of the Edwardian period? Partially, yes, but only partially. Some of the patterns appear too frequently to be unconscious; Conrad was too aware of his own art to leave major themes and symbols to chance. In any case, his fiction employs an impressive number of Wagnerian patterns, but we have lost much of the background of the Edwardians and often do not recognize these patterns when they occur. I shall point them out in Conrad's fiction and show that the composer was their real source.

The condition of Joseph Conrad's published correspondence is indeed sad; there is no complete edition of his letters and there is certainly a need for one. Edward Garnett's edition is the most complete, but hundreds of letters are not included in it. Many of them may have been lost, since we know that Conrad wrote many more letters than we have in collections or in print. However, from the published letters to Marguerite Poradowska the following quotation is highly significant. Conrad was working on *Almayer's Folly* at the time and in May 1894 he wrote to her: "*Je Vous enverrai bientôt le dernier Chap.: Il commence avec un trio Nina, Dain, Almayer, et il finit dans un long solo pour Almayer qui est presque aussi long que le Tristan-solo de Wagner*."[2] This passage is interesting because of its use of the musical terms *trio* and *solo*, which suggest that Conrad used musical ideas to structure his fiction. Also the reference to the Tristan solo in Wagner, which must refer to Tristan's long monologue at the beginning of Act III, implies a real knowledge of the opera. Conrad mentions the composer again in a letter to William Blackwood dated May 31, 1902. He has been discussing various Victorian novelists like Scott, Thackeray, and George Eliot, then contrasts them with his own approach to the novel: "But these are great names. I don't compare myself with them. I am modern, and I would rather recall Wagner the musician and Rodin the sculptor."[3] This quotation is significant because it draws an analogy with Wagnerian music rather than with literature. These are the only direct references to the composer that I can find in Conrad's printed correspondence, yet both are more than passing comments and indicate a real awareness of the operas.

Wagnerism was an integral part of the intellectual milieu of Edwardian England and Conrad was too aware of his time to ignore it. As Paul L. Wiley has said: "Conrad's knowledge of Flaubert is merely one indication of the broader relationship between his art and the literary and intellectual background of the 1890's and the earlier years of the present century, the period to which the bulk of his writing belongs. Since he was alert to the temper of the age, a closer study than is possible here of this aspect of his work might well bring light to bear upon the traces in his fiction of the contemporary interest in Schopenhauer, Nietzsche, Wagner, in socialism and feminism, in religious and scientific controversy."[4] We know that Covent Garden was staging Wagnerian opera often during the 90s and the Edwardian period, that many intellectuals and artists were going to these performances and to Bayreuth, and that Conrad was aware of all this. Moreover, Conrad had several musical friends who were very fond of opera; Galsworthy, Bennett, and Ford are among these, but Ford was Conrad's most probable link to Wagnerian opera.

Ford Madox Ford was the son of Francis Hueffer, who had left Germany but remained an ardent Wagnerian throughout his life. He wrote the first book on Wagner in English and was the editor of an influential Wagnerian journal called *Die Meister*. Because of all this activity poor Ford got to see very little of his father; the boy was sent off to a boarding school at an early age and during the summers his father went to Bayreuth, the Wagner Mecca. Although emotionally neglected by his father, Ford did absorb a great knowledge of the composer from him. *The Nature of a Crime*, according to Bernard Meyer and several other critics, is the most obviously Wagnerian of his works.[5] This novel was a collaboration of both Ford and Conrad, but Ford wrote most of it. It is significant that such a knowledgeable Wagnerian was Conrad's literary collaborator as well as a close friend. Meyer, in his psychological study of Conrad, claims that this was one of the most important relationships in the author's life, both personally and artistically. The men not only wrote novels together but, perhaps more important, theorized about the nature of their art. The loss of Ford's friendship was a major loss for Conrad. In his *Joseph Conrad: A Personal Remembrance* Ford does not say much about the musical roots of Conrad's art, but he does relate an incident that took place during the heyday of their collaboration. Ford is describing here their difficulties during a short trip they and their families took together: "The most terrible struggles of all took place in a windy hotel at Knocke on the Belgian coast, with a contralto from Bayreuth practicing in the basement. Her voice literally shook the flimsy house. Whilst we wrote or groaned on the fourth floor the glasses on a tray jarred together in sympathy with the contralto passages of 'Die Götterdämmerung.' . . . Conrad was then beginning 'Nostromo' in the mornings.''[6] Conrad was hearing *Die Götterdämmerung* in the background as he began work on *Nostromo*, according to Ford. We shall see that the *Ring* had a marked effect upon that novel.

But aside from personal and historical influences, music itself was central to Conrad's theory of the novel. The passage that is usually quoted in any discussion of his awareness of music is from the preface to *The Nigger of the ''Narcissus''*: ''All art, therefore, appeals primarily to the senses, and the artistic aim when expressing itself in written words must also make its appeal through the senses, if its high desire is to reach the secret spring of responsive emotions. It must strenuously aspire to the plasticity of sculpture, to the color of painting, and to the magic suggestiveness of music—which is the art of arts.''[7] Such exalted praise of music is clearly relevant to this discussion. There was, it must be remembered, a tradition for this in the Edwardian period that originated with the Victorians. Walter Pater became famous for his statement about the supremacy of music among the arts, and the theory became accepted by most of the aesthetes and decadents. Many of these people were also Wagnerites. Oscar Wilde, George Moore, Aubrey Beardsley, and Swinburne were all Wagnerians in their musical taste; several of them also consciously imitated Wagner's musical and dramatic effects in their writing, as I have mentioned in the introduction. But, as with so much of the aesthetic theory of this period, the roots are to be found in France. Most of the French Symbolist poets were devotees of Wagner and this appreciation extended to both his music and librettos. Donald Yelton, writing of Conrad's knowledge of music, contrasts it with that of some of his French contemporaries: ''Conrad had none of the musical sophistication of a Proust or a Thomas Mann; he had, unlike Gide, no musical avocation . . . . Of musical knowledge he probably had less even than Baudelaire or Mallarmé, both professed Wagnerians . . . . Yet the Preface [to the *Nigger*] speaks of music as 'the art of arts'; and whether the passage consciously echoes Pater's familiar dictum or some remembered fragment of *Symboliste* prose, or whether it expressed an original intuition, Conrad's musical reference is, in its context, of great suggestive value for an approach to his fiction."[8] What the French Symbolists admired most about music was its suggestiveness, and they aimed for this quality in their literary work. The "magic suggestiveness of music" attracted Conrad too, and he used references to music, as did the aesthetes and French Symbolists, to create musical qualities in his fiction.

In addition to his desire for musical effects, Conrad was also very much interested in myth. Many of his characters are archetypal heroes in epic opposition to enemies often described as personifications of the evil in the universe. Many of his situations suggest ancient ritual rather than what happens in real life. Thus, the San Tomé silver is not just a metal; Ricardo, Jones, and Pedro are not simply three nasty people who happen to be traveling together; and Captain Fidanza is not merely a greedy Italian. Conrad's artistic imagination naturally saw characters and situations in terms of mythic conflict and in this he is very similar to the German composer, whose operas display the combination of music and myth that Conrad sought in his writing. Except for Wagner's first three pieces of juvenilia, all of his operas are based on medieval legends or old German epics like the *Nibelungenlied*. His music-dramas aimed for the combination of music and myth that he admired in Greek tragedy.[9] Given Conrad's interest in myth, as well as his desire for musical effects in his prose, he was inevitably attracted to Wagnerian opera.

Since Conrad himself mentions Wagner in connection with his first novel, *Almayer's Folly* (1895), we can begin there. In that letter to Marguerite Poradowska, Conrad says he is working on the last chapter of the novel and that it "begins with a *trio*—Nina, Dain, Almayer—and ends with a long *solo* for Almayer which is almost as long as Tristan's in Wagner." There is a musical quality about the last chapter, and indeed the whole novel, that justifies Conrad's use of musical terminology like *trio* and *solo*. The chapter opens with a triolike exchange between Almayer, his daughter Nina, and Dain that is musical in its cadences but not noticeably Wagnerian. The chapter also includes an immolation scene, which is highly reminiscent of the conclusion of the *Ring*, when Almayer burns down his old house after taking a final look at Nina's clothing and few remaining belongings. The rest of the chapter relates the decline and death of the fated Almayer and ends with a highly ironic reference by Abdulla to "Allah the Compassionate." Conrad wrote to his Polish relative that this chapter reminded him of Tristan's long solo, which must refer to Tristan's long monologue at the beginning and continuing into the middle of the last act of the opera. There Tristan curses his fate, curses the love potion that Brangaene switched for the death potion, and wishes he were dead. By the third act of the opera he is fatally wounded, in pain, and delirious, and wishes for Isolde to end his misery. When her ship is finally sighted he yearns for her as well as death and gets both when he tears off his bandages and dies just as she reaches him. There is suicidal motivation in Almayer's final actions as well, for his pathetic insistence on trying to forget Nina and his wretched past is really a desire for the forgetfulness that only death can provide. In his desperation to annihilate his memories he even resorts to opium, hoping to find there the peace that his life cannot provide. Conrad's description of him in death reinforces the Tristan-like effect he said he had tried to create: "On the upturned face there was that serene look which follows the sudden relief from anguish and pain, and it testified silently before the cloudless heaven that the man lying there under the gaze of indifferent eyes had been permitted to forget before he died."[10] Like Tristan after his painful solo in the last act of the opera, Almayer has found his peace and forgetfulness, but only in death. The slow-moving cadence of this long, balanced sentence, typical of many in the last chapter, adds to the musical quality of the novel's ending.

Much of the imagery of the novel is also highly reminiscent of *Tristan*. The repeated references to light, dark, and water could have come directly from the opera. In that work, darkness is always a shield for the lovers, while light is inimical to them. Tristan tells Isolde during the *Liebesnacht* that only in night can he find peace with her, but the day and the sun will destroy them. The lovers are caught together at the dawn and Tristan dies under bright sunlight. Moreover, the first act takes place on an ocean voyage from Ireland to Cornwall and it is on the sea that they declare their love. By the last act Tristan is again by the shores of the ocean and looking for Isolde's ship. One of the major symbols in *Almayer's Folly* is the river that the lovers paddle along and meet upon: it protects and shelters them and hides their love from the other characters. They usually meet at night, for the darkness also protects them; during the day they must not show their love to the others. This pattern of darkness, used consistently, appears finally when Nina leaves her father for Dain's homeland: "The canoe disappeared, and Almayer stood motionless with his eyes fixed on its wake . . . . As the sun declined, the sea-breeze sprang up from the northward and shivered with its breath the glassy surface of the water" (p. 194). This is the last we, and Almayer, see of them and the increasing darkness of the setting sun is an important part of this final tableau; significantly, water is mentioned here too. The lighting creates an aura of death and doom, as it has done consistently in the novel. The dim light of the setting sun suggests that Nina will not live happily ever after, that perhaps she will ultimately become just another part of Dain's harem. Of course this is hardly the tragic ending of *Tristan und Isolde*, but Conrad's use of lighting and water imagery parallels the opera and creates a somber atmosphere for the lovers and the probable future of their love.

Another of the basic symbols in the novel is its dark forest. It is consistently portrayed as an evil, dangerous force that gives shelter but also entangles, and at one point it almost traps the lovers when the Dutch come upon them. The eleventh chapter, which describes

Dain waiting for Nina in the forest, begins with the following description: "On three sides of the clearing, appearing very far away in the deceptive light, the big trees of the forest, lashed together with manifold bonds by a mass of tangled creepers, looked down at the growing young life at their feet with the sombre resignation of giants that had lost faith in their strength. And in the midst of them the merciless creepers clung to the big trunks in cable-like coils, leaped from tree to tree, hung in thorny festoons from the lower boughs, and sending slender tendrils on high to seek out the smallest branches, carried death to their victims in an exulting riot of silent destruction" (p. 165). There are several other passages that describe the forest in equally sardonic and mysterious terms. Its dark, "deceptive light" adds to the ominous atmosphere of the novel. This is clearly no ordinary forest but a lushly tropical, evil, and highly symbolical one. Paul L. Wiley, in *Conrad's Measure of Man*, sees a Wagnerian analogy here: "Heavy mythical and somewhat Wagnerian undertones accompany the narrative of Almayer's decline, as though the Amfortas legend had been transferred to a Klingsor's garden of Bornean jungle in which a Malay Parsifal, Dain Maroola, falls victim to desire and plays renegade rather than savior."[11] Klingsor's magic garden in the second act of *Parsifal*, like the forest in *Almayer's Folly*, represents the evil in the world, which tries to trap the innocent and naive. There Kundry tries to seduce Parsifal and thereby destroy his innocent goodness; her lushly tropical background mirrors her (and Klingsor's) evil intentions. Such a connection gives the forest in the novel a more suggestive atmosphere of abstract evil. "A Smile of Fortune," we shall see later, uses the Magic Garden reference more centrally and exactly. This reference in *Almayer's Folly*, like those to *Tristan*, is consistent with Conrad's aim of "suggestiveness" for the novel; Wagnerian patterns help him to hint at whole realms of myth and music that elevate the novel above a solely realistic treatment of a sordid story to a mythic tale of love, entrapment, and death.

Conrad used the *Tristan und Isolde* framework once again, but with greater fidelity, in a short story written a year after *Almayer's Folly*. "The Lagoon," which was published in 1897, almost exactly echoes the Wagnerian treatment of the myth in atmosphere and symbolism. The death of the woman at the end of the story occurs by the sea and just as the sun rises. The equation of death with light and love with night and darkness, combined with the sea's role as seeming protector of the lovers, parallels exactly the Wagnerian version of the story. The fact that the lovers escape at the expense of the life of Arsat's brother provides an initial evil omen that marks their love with death from the beginning. As Arsat tells the white man: "My brother! Three times he called—but I was not afraid of life. Was she not there in that canoe? And could I not with her find a country where death is forgotten—where death is unknown."[12] Arsat's belief in a love beyond death is as firm as Tristan's.

The lagoon itself is described frequently and its presence is clearly symbolical. "Over the lagoon a mist drifting and low had crept, erasing slowly the glittering images of the stars. And now a great expanse of white vapour covered the land: it flowed cold and gray in the darkness, eddied in noiseless whirls round the tree-trunks and about the platform of the house, which seemed to float upon a restless and impalpable illusion of a sea. Only far away the tops of the trees stood outlined on the twinkle of heaven, like a sombre and forbidding shore—a coast deceptive, pitiless and black" (p. 201). The misty lagoon suggests the real world, which the lovers had hoped to escape. The water becomes mist and actually engulfs the land so that it too seems sea, while the dark and murky quality of the eddying lagoon and its forbidding shore of trees suggest that death will force itself upon the couple despite their love. The sea invades and obliterates the land, just as death overcomes the lovers; the sea's seeming protection is illusory.

It is symbolically appropriate that the girl dies with the dawn, since darkness is always connected with their love. The following passage describes the scene immediately after the girl's death: "in the merciless sunshine the whisper of unconscious life grew

Though Conrad frequently referred to *Tristan und Isolde*, "Falk" (1903) indicates that he was also aware of Wagner's other works. Once again I am indebted to Paul Wiley for pointing out the operatic element in the story: "In 'Falk' Conrad had touched on the redeeming power of sympathy in the love of Hermann's niece for the suffering mariner in a tale slightly reminiscent of Wagner's *Flying Dutchman* theme."[13] The Vanderdecken in Conrad's tale is Falk, a tugboat captain who often says how lonely he is and wishes he had a wife. But his curse seems to be that he cannot find a woman who will live with him. His very solitude has put a gloomy silence about him that repels most people; he has been alone for so long that he no longer knows how to communicate with them. But as the story progresses we find that the real curse he is living under, which forces him into his gloomy solitude, is the fact of his past cannibalism, and Hermann's shocked, disgusted reaction is the usual response to Falk's disclosure. The narrator's partially sympathetic hearing of the grisly details of the incident gives the reader the whole story. Yet, says the narrator, Falk is basically a domestic man who wants to find a wife. In Wagnerian terms he is looking for a Senta whose steadfast love can break his curse of isolation.

The Senta he finds and falls in love with is Hermann's niece. Significantly, Conrad never gives her a name; usually she is simply referred to as "Hermann's niece," who lives with his family on board the *Diana*. She is consistently described as a sexy girl, very shapely and buxom. And her silence is more total than Falk's, for she does not speak one line throughout the story, which creates a similarity of sorts between them. But her effect, despite her silence, is clearly electric upon Falk as well as the narrator. "She was the tender and voiceless siren of this appalling navigator. He evidently wanted to live his whole conception of life. Nothing else would do. And she, too, was a servant of that life that, in the midst of death, cries aloud to our senses. She was eminently fitted to interpret for him its feminine side. And in her own way, and with her own profusion of sensuous charms, she also seemed to illustrate the eternal truth of an unerring principle."[14] The abstract and mythic tone of this description parallels Wagner's treatment of the Dutchman story as a conflict of life and death. This Senta, like Wagner's, is true to her Flying Dutchman captain, and like Wagner's she has to fight her family to do it. They try to stop her but she is determined, for her heart has gone out to the Dutchman and his solitude. The story, like the opera, has the happy resolution of redemption through love, for the curse is lifted: the two solitary beings are joined and mated and their solitude, if not their silence, is dispelled. The sea is also a pervasive element in both works and both sets of characters have nautical backgrounds. Wagner's Senta prefers the sea-faring Dutchman to Erik, a hunter, and Conrad's heroine is also a creature of the sea.

There is also much comedy in Wagner's opera—in its folksy music for the Norwegian sailors, the character of Mary, and the giggling spinning girls—and this too is reflected in Conrad's story. Primarily because of the narrator and his penchant for cynical asides, much of the story's tone is comic. Early in "Falk" the narrator describes Hermann's ship as the height of domesticity, complete with four children and a clothesline for the family wash; yet it is named the *Diana*. As the narrator comments: "This ridiculously unsuitable name struck one as an impertinence towards the memory of the most charming of goddesses" (p. 149). The narrator's remarks are also used to destroy any possible seriousness when he first tells Hermann of Falk's desire to marry his niece. Hermann left in such a hurry, says the narrator, that he "had barely the time, as he made for the cabin door, to grab him by the seat of his inexpressibles" (p. 213). Falk's dramatic confession of his past act of eating a man is also deflated by Hermann's shocked reply: "Himmel! What for?" (p. 218). Such a commonsensical answer breaks the dramatic mood and results in comedy. When Falk relates the grisly details of his man-eating, the narrator once again wrecks the impending seriousness by interjecting: "Why continue the story of that ship, that story before which . . . the fable of the *Flying Dutchman* with its convention of crime and its sentimental retribution fades like a graceful wreath, like a wisp of white mist. What is there to say that everyone of us cannot guess for himself?" (pp. 234-35). Such a sudden interruption, with its sarcastic comparison of the story with another famous sea myth, effectively destroys any possibility of tragedy. That this myth is precisely the one Conrad has been alluding to adds to the ironic quality of the comment. The narrator even ends the story waggishly when he relates that Falk left the port five years later but that the town was still busy gossiping about the man "who had won his wife at cards from the captain of an English ship" (p. 240). Thanks to comments such as these, the narrator has created a comic tone in the story that cleverly reflects its Wagnerian referent.

The year after "Falk" appeared, Conrad published what most critics feel is his greatest novel, *Nostromo* (1904). Several of them have noticed its Wagnerian parallels, which give it the kind of "suggestiveness" Conrad sought. Once again I am indebted to Paul L. Wiley, who was one of the first to disclose this connection: "The curse attached to the silver is as productive of fatal consequences as that upon the stolen gold in Wagner's *Ring*, for avarice not only defeats the protagonists in the novel but also excludes love as a redeeming force."[15] Wiley makes two separate points here, both of which I shall investigate: first, the silver is a thing accursed, and second, it destroys love in those who seek it. As Bernard Shaw pointed out in 1898 in *The Perfect Wagnerite*, this is exactly how the gold operates in the *Ring*. The Rhinemaidens make abundantly clear right in the first scene of *Das Rheingold* that the power of the ring will come only to the person who can renounce love. The ugly Nibelung Alberich immediately decides to do this and with his new-found power tyrannizes his brother Mime and the other Nibelung dwarfs. But the real horror of the ring's power is its awesome ability to corrupt the good as well as the evil. If Alberich were the only one entranced with the ring, the effect would still be terrible but not subtle. But the tragedy in Wagner's *Ring* occurs when even a good and great man, Wotan, is corrupted by the ring and willing to plot and kill to possess it and the total dominance it will bring.

All this relates directly to Conrad's *Nostromo*, and the connection is too close to be coincidental. The similarity between Wagner's *Ring* and this novel creates a mythically suggestive dimension in *Nostromo*. It is significant that the San Tomé silver mine is first mentioned while Conrad is describing the young love and courtship of the Goulds in Italy. Early in her married life Emilia becomes aware of an evil shadow darkening her happiness with her husband: "Mrs. Gould knew the history of the San Tomé mine. Worked in the early days mostly by means of lashes on the backs of slaves, its yield had been paid for in its own weight of human bones. Whole tribes of Indians had perished in the exploitation; and then the mine was abandoned, since with this primitive method it had ceased to make a profitable return no matter how many corpses were thrown in its maw. Then it became forgotten. It was rediscovered after the War of Independence."[16] The irony in the last sentence is a typical Conradian touch. The mine, ominously connected with death, poses a threat to the Goulds' new love. This connection is also reinforced by the fact that Charles first hears of his father's death while he is courting Emilia in Italy. He believes that the silver mine had hounded his father to an early grave; that this death should occur while he is first in love parallels the curse in Wagner's *Ring*.

Charles Gould's father did not want the mine; it was foisted on him by one of Costaguana's more corrupt politicians, who wanted the rents for himself. The effects of the mine upon the elder Gould soon became apparent: "'It will end by killing me,' he used to affirm many times a day. And, in fact, since that time he began to suffer from fever, from liver pains, and mostly from a worrying inability to think of anything else . . . . He implored his son never to return to Costaguana, never to claim any part of his inheritance there, because it was tainted by the infamous Concession" (pp. 56-57). But Charles decided to ignore his father's warning and returns to Costaguana with his new wife. At the beginning of their marriage Charles and Emilia are happily in love and eager for the excitement of a new adventure, but by the end of the novel they are a loveless couple without children. Toward the end Mrs. Gould asks herself: "What more could she have expected? . . . Love was only a short moment of forgetfulness, a short intoxication, whose delight one remembered with a sense of sadness, as if it had been a deep grief lived through . . . . She saw the San Tomé mountain hanging over the Campo, over the whole land, feared, hated, wealthy, more soulless than any tyrant, more pitiless and autocratic than the worst government, ready to crush innumberable lives in the expansion of its greatness . . . . A terrible success for the last of the Goulds. The last! She had hoped for a long, long time, that perhaps— But no! There were to be no more. An immense desolation, the dread of her own continued life, descended upon the first lady of Sulaco" (pp. 521-22). The young wife happily in love has become the sad and lonely mature woman without children and without the love of her husband, and she rightly blames the central obsession of her husband's life for this situation, the silver mine.

Charles Gould has also changed from a young man in love, when we first see him, to a mechanical but powerful bureaucrat whose life is completely circumscribed by his *idée fixe*, his silver mine. On many occasions he spends the night at the mine rather than with his lonely wife, and at one point he is even willing to blow it up lest someone else gain possession of it. Like Wagner's Wotan, Charles Gould is a good and occasionally great man, with a naive belief in the powers of what he is seeking. Wotan thinks that when he possesses the ring, by whatever means, a new era of peace and justice will reign in the universe, just as surely as Charles Gould believes that material interests alone will solve all of mankind's social and economic problems. By the end of the novel he has become a mindless capitalist who sleeps with his true mistress, his mine. As Winifred Lynskey has generalized: "The novel reveals what all of Conrad's novels reveal: that evil is too powerful for humanity".[17] Charles Gould's corruption is as total as Wotan's.

Such a pessimistic view of the force and power of evil is common to both the *Ring* and the novel. Both also use a large and even epic scope to communicate their visions of gloom and death. Wagner needed a tetralogy of operas to tell his tale and Conrad's *Nostromo* is also a large work with epic dimensions. E. M. W. Tillyard spends a whole chapter on the novel in his *The Epic Strain in the English Novel*. He comments on its large scope in the following passage: "It is unique among all of the works of Conrad in its span, both of space and of time .... The main action takes place within three days, but simultaneously is set in a great stretch of history with hints of prehistory or of the fabulous. These matters are vital in creating the epic effect."[18] This epic effect is evident in the implications of the corruption of Charles Gould, but he is hardly the only one corrupted by material interests. Captain Fidanza's fatal downfall is also a result of greed for the silver and here again we have a good man, worlds apart from the desperate and Alberich-like greed of Sotillo. Nostromo is a capable man, much admired by the people of Sulaco; yet for him, too, the choice of love or money presents itself and he chooses money.

We have seen that Gould's father considered the silver mine accursed and that this parallels the curse that Alberich puts upon the ring in *Das Rheingold*. Nostromo's own doom is also prophesied by a curse of which he is painfully aware. Teresa Viola is the ominous figure here, for she dislikes his vanity and pride and predicts his downfall. On her deathbed, certainly a dramatic moment, she tells him: "They have turned your head with their praises .... Your folly shall betray you into poverty, misery, starvation. The very leperos shall laugh at you—the great Capataz" (p. 257). He remembers this curse when he is first approached by Dr. Monygham with the idea of getting the last load of treasure out of Sulaco before Sotillo can get it. He retorts: "It is as if I were taking a curse upon me, Senor Doctor. A man with a treasure on this coast will have every knife raised against him in every place upon the shore. You see that, Senor Doctor? I shall float along with a spell upon my life" (p. 259). Nostromo interprets the curse as a threat of death and, significantly, this is exactly how it finally affects him. The treasure that he thought would bring him so much happiness finally denies him both life and love. Toward the end of the novel we can see the silver's insidious effects upon the once glorious and noble capataz: "Nostromo had lost his peace; the genuineness of all his qualities was destroyed. He felt it himself, and often cursed the silver of San Tomé. His courage, his magnificence, his leisure, his work, everything was as before, only everything was a sham. But the treasure was real" (pp. 523-24). The money has become the only reality for the capataz and slavery is not an exaggerated analogy. Conrad uses it himself: "He could never shake off the treasure. His audacity, greater than that of other men, had welded that vein of silver into his life. And the feeling of fearful and ardent subjection, the feeling of slavery . . . weighed heavily on the independent Captain Fidanza" (pp. 526-527).

His subjection to his money infects his capacity to love as well, which parallels events in the *Ring*. Alberich's curse of death and the Rhinemaidens' description of the loss of love are both combined in Captain Fidanza's downfall. Thus, he visits Giselle Viola on the Great Isabel only after he digs up more of his treasure. The sick desperation of his love for her is evident in the following passage: "Her form drooped consolingly over the low casement towards the slave of the unlawful treasure. The light in the room went out, and, weighted with silver, the magnificent capataz clasped her round her white neck in the darkness of the gulf as a drowning man clutches at a straw" (pp. 544-45). Both aspects of the curse are operating in this passage, loss of love and life. Giselle begs him to take her away and forget the treasure, but Fidanza will have nothing to do with this plan. When he is finally shot by old Viola, he recognizes at once his mistake and the power of the accursed treasure. His dying words make this very clear: "The Spell is broken! . . . The silver has killed me" (pp. 558-59). Like Mrs. Gould, Giselle Viola has been abandoned for money; the connection is made explicit when Emilia tries to comfort her: "'Console yourself, child. Very soon he would have forgotten you for his treasure.' 'Senora, he loved me. He loved me,' Giselle whispered, despairingly. 'He loved me as no one had ever been loved before.' 'I have been loved too,' Mrs. Gould said, in a severe tone'' (p. 561).

The ending of the novel is clearly not realistic, but uses an operatic atmosphere to create the ''staged ending'' that Conrad was so fond of. The final sentence in the novel repeats for the last time the central theme of love versus money. Dr. Monygham is rowing from the Great Isabel back to Sulaco after Nostromo's death when he sees over the dark Golfo Placido a sight that reminds him of both the silver and the dead Nostromo: '' . . . a big white cloud shining like a mass of solid silver, the genius of the magnificent capataz de cargadores dominated the dark gulf containing his conquests of treasure and love'' (p. 566). The last three words of the novel summarize its basic conflict, and that conflict also operates in Wagner's *Ring*. But here again the setting, lighting, and commentary create both the staged ending and operatic rather than realistic atmosphere that is at the center of Conrad's theory of literature.

In both *Nostromo* and the *Ring* there are many deaths and destroyed loves, which create a pervasive gloom that colors the atmospheres of both the novel and the operas. Significantly, both works also end with a vision of water. The last page of the novel describes a white cloud over the gulf on the night of Nostromo's death; the *Ring* ends where it began, in the waters of the Rhine. In both works the water suggests a baptismal attempt to wash away some of the greed and evil that have been described. Redemption through love, the mighty Wagnerian theme of the *Ring*, is the promised cleansing agent in *Nostromo* as well. The lighthouse at the end of the novel reinforces this positive effect. The only force pitted against the power of the silver is love, and for the two major characters in the novel a kind of redemption does occur. Charles Gould is still loved by his wife, even if he is incapable of responding, and Nostromo has become a living legend in Sulaco, which is a social redemption. But neither Emilia nor Giselle, unlike Brünnhilde at the end of *Götterdämmerung*, have immolation scenes;

their heroes either die or somehow carry on as before. Conradian tragedy portrays people who are forewarned but incapable of avoiding their doom. Just as Wagner's Wotan knows early in the *Ring* that he is fated, so Nostromo fears the curse of the silver from its departure from Sulaco, yet is unable to avoid the outcome. He may curse his own position as thief and slave, but he cannot escape it—rather like a fly unto a wanton god. Both Conrad and Wagner have justifiably been accused of determinism in their characterization.

How does *Nostromo* benefit from its Wagnerian parallels? Primarily they help Conrad create the epic effect he wants; the many correspondences to Wagnerian opera add to the epic quality of his novel. Thus, Charles Gould's character has been elevated through the comparison with Wotan; the importance of the silver is heightened when compared to the corrupting gold of the *Ring*; and the major conflicts in the novel become more apparent and more forceful when seen through its Wagnerian patterns. Both situations and characters are clarified and made more epic because of these mythic connections, and these patterns also help Conrad end his novel effectively. Many critics have accused its last chapters of melodrama, but seen through a Wagnerian framework the ending is staged, nonrealistic, and atmospherically mythic. The connections with Wagner's mythic operas save the situation from becoming melodramatic; instead Captain Fidanza and his love are portrayed as the final fated victims of the silver.

In 1912 three of Conrad's longer tales were published together under the title *'Twixt Land and Sea*; several critics have noticed the Wagnerian patterns in two of them. Edward Said's brief discussion of the first is helpful: "'A Smile of Fortune,' the story of a young English captain's delay on a small Pacific island, his encounter with Alice Jacobus, a sensual creature, whose strange father has an equally strange brother, takes place largely in Alice's beautiful garden. Alice's long hair, the almost unconscious beguilements she practices on the innocent hero, the climactic kiss the hero gives the girl—all of these suggest the enactment of a Pacific *Parsifal*, with Alice playing Kundry to the hero's Parsifal.''[19] The story itself contrasts two worlds: the masculine and more wholesome world of the sea in opposition to the tempting, earthly ''Pearl of the Pacific'' island. The mariners in the story can be compared to the Grail brotherhood in *Parsifal* and Wagner's hero is very similar to Conrad's naive narrator; both are ''*Tor*'' or innocents. Both are also tempted by women to betray their brotherhood and the temptations in both works occur in a magic garden. There is certainly something peculiar and witchlike about Alice Jacobus, like Wagner's Kundry, and her father is Klingsor-like in his greedy mercantilism. Conrad's description of Alice in her garden is strikingly similar to Kundry in her magic garden during the second act of the opera: ''I looked her over, from the top of her dishevelled head, down the lovely line of the shoulder, following the curve of the hip, the draped form of the long limb, right down to her fine ankle below a torn, soiled flounce; and as far as the point of the shabby, high-heeled, blue slipper, dangling from her well-shaped foot, which she moved slightly, with quick, nervous jerks, as if impatient of my presence. And in the scent of the massed flowers I seemed to breathe her special and inexplicable charm, the heady perfume of the everlastingly irritated captive of the garden.''[20] Alice's garden is not just a background but a part of her forceful attraction, which is how the magic garden operates for Kundry. Alice always seems to be vanishing into and out of space, like some supernatural creature. She is a strange kind of tease who is nasty but always appealing, and her witchlike characterization is reinforced by the presence of her ferocious governess. Alice's very isolation and loneliness appeal to the hero's sympathies and he naively imagines himself a rescuer. Within a perfumed and beautiful garden the narrator is tempted by these strange, unhappy women, for the father can find no one to marry his daughter; but, like Parsifal, the narrator avoids these snares and remains true to the masculine code of the sea. Despite the Klingsor-like plotting of old Jacobus to tempt the boy into marrying his crazy daughter, the narrator avoids this trap and escapes.

But he does not escape unscathed, because he has learned something about human suffering and has lost his youthful innocence. His thoughts as his ship leaves the Pearl of the Pacific harbor reflect this change: "I was glad enough to be at sea, but not with the gladness of old days. Formerly I had no memories to take away with me. I shared in the blessed forgetfulness of sailors, that forgetfulness natural and invincible, which resembles innocence in so far that it prevents self-examination. Now however I remembered the girl" (p. 82). His contact with that strange girl has made him aware of human suffering and as a result he has lost his naivete. This parallels exactly Wagner's version of the myth, for in Act I Guernemanz says that the Grail Brotherhood can be saved only by: "*Durch Mitleid wissend, der reine Tor*" (the pure innocent made wise through pity). By the last act of the opera Parsifal is no longer an innocent fool, for his encounter in the magic garden has taught him pity for suffering. The passage above indicates that the narrator in this story has gone through the same process of suffering and wisdom. His ship's ominous cargo of seventeen tons of rotting potatoes are there to remind us of those aspects of humanity he had been unaware of. This pattern of innocence and new knowledge occurs in Wagner's version of the Parsifal myth, as we have seen, but not in any others. Neither Malory's version, nor Jessie Weston's in *From Ritual to Romance*, describes Parsifal as a character of central importance who goes through this symbolical passage from innocence through human pity to wisdom. We can conclude, then, that Wagner's *Parsifal* is the most probable source for the legend as it appears in "A Smile of Fortune." The story has gained a mythic dimension because of the connection and the narrator is elevated from a particular young man to a kind of nautical Everyboy. The pattern is Jungian and archetypal in both works.

"Freya of the Seven Isles" is the most obviously Wagnerian of Conrad's works. It is the only story in which Wagner is mentioned specifically in the text, but the allusion is hardly necessary for anyone who knows *Tristan und Isolde*. That the tale is about love is told us immediately in the title, for Freya was the Nordic goddess of love. Conrad's Freya, like Wagner's Isolde, is a very tempestuous woman who also happens to be fond of the sea. As the narrator comments: "I don't know whether she was actually born at sea, but I do know that up to twelve years of age she sailed about with her parents in various ships" (p. 150). The association of this woman with the sea is significant because of its parallel with Wagner's Isolde. Just as water imagery pervades that opera, so it does Conrad's story. Another aspect of Freya's character is shown by her choice of music: "Freya would sit down to the piano and play fierce Wagner music in the flicker of blinding flashes, with thunderbolts falling all round, enough to make your hair stand on end" (p. 152). In fact, she uses this same music to taunt Heemskirk when he comes to court her. Although in the beginning Jasper Allen is not very similar to Wagner's world-weary Tristan, their endings are alike. Both commit suicide in rather grim and desperate fashion; Tristan by ripping off his bandages and Allen "by cutting his throat in the house of a half-caste with whom he had been lodging since he came ashore from the wreck" (p. 231). His death has a shattering effect upon Freya, and her death as a result of losing him is within the Wagnerian framework as well. It is appropriate that Freya's last words in the story refer to the sea: "Draw the curtain, Papa. Shut the sea out. It reproaches me with my folly" (p. 238). Conrad's connection of Freya's love with the sea is ominous, given the way he usually dramatizes it. The sea can be kind and beautiful, but can just as easily be fierce and deadly; while at sea Allen loses his brig to Heemskirk and the Dutch authorities. The water imagery for the love, together with the allusion to Wagner's *Tristan*, warn us immediately of the eventual fate of the lovers.

As is his frequent practice, Conrad uses a narrator in "Freya." The story begins with him and immediately gives us an insight into his character: "One day—and that day was many years ago now—I received a long, chatty letter from one of my old chums and fellow-wanderers in Eastern waters" (p. 147). This light, conversational tone, typical of him, serves to balance the highly emotional and fatal events in the story. I suspect that Conrad feared that the love story might become too operatic without some distancing device like a narrator. The narrator tends to be ironic and comic in his observations of the action, at least in the beginning. Early in the story, when Freya and Jasper are alone together in her father's house, the narrator waggishly describes them as "amusing themselves very quietly, and no doubt very heartily" (p. 156). Only toward the end does he display much emotion, when even he is moved by old Nelson's pathetic attempts to believe that his daughter died of pneumonia rather than love. "Man!" says the narrator, "don't you see that she died of it?" (p. 238). His ironic distance is gone by the end of the story.

In *Chance* (1913), as in "Falk," Conrad uses patterns of imagery and characterization from *Der Fliegende Holländer*. That opera distinguishes between land people and sea people, and Wagner suggests that they lead two very different ways of life with separate experiences and values. The main narrator in *Chance*, Marlow, makes this distinction early in the novel. "Little Fyne," Marlow's strange friend, is the quintessential landlubber who loves to hike all over the country, while Marlow detests this kind of exercise. When he describes Fyne, he contrasts himself to him in the following passage: "You know how I hate walking—at least on solid-rural earth; for I can walk a ship's deck a whole foggy night through, if necessary, and think little of it."[21] The landlubber versus the man of the sea is the basic conflict in the novel, and the decision to set out to sea rather neatly divides the novel in two and gives it a form that reflects its two categories of people.

This contrast between people of the land and people of the sea suggests more than just place of birth or current occupation. Conrad, like Wagner, meant to imply something about a state of mind peculiar to both kinds of existence. The division is sustained throughout the novel, but only toward the end does Conrad become explicit about exact differences. In the last third of the novel Marlow generalizes about marriage quarrels and their source: "If you ask me what is an ordinary marital quarrel I will tell you that it is a difference about nothing; I mean, these nothings which, as Mr. Powell told us when we first met him, shore people are so prone to start a row about, and nurse into hatred from an idle sense of wrong, from perverted ambition, for spectacular reasons too'' (p. 326). This passage, in part, dramatizes Marlow's bachelor cynicism about marriage in general, but I believe that a more serious theme is also present. Conrad suggests here, and elsewhere in the novel, that shore people are more prone to worry about petty concerns and materialistic ambitions than sea people. He not only states this but dramatizes it in characters like the obtuse Fynes and the materialistic old De Barral.

Sea people tend to live beyond mundane concerns because the steady contemplation of the lonely sea brings them, Conrad implies, a greater sense of human solitude and even a metaphysical awareness of the universe. Of course every generalization includes its opposite, but this one does appear several times in *Chance*. It occurs when Marlow describes Fyne's final encounter with Captain Anthony: ''Captain Anthony—as far as I could gather from little Fyne—had meant well. As far as such lofty words may be applied to the obscure personages of this story, we were all filled with the noblest sentiments and intentions. The sea was there to give them the shelter of its solitude free from the earth's petty suggestions'' (pp. 309-10). Even young Powell becomes aware of this quality of the sea on his first voyage in the *Ferndale*. His thoughts on night watch are described in the following passage: ''The serenity of the peaceful night seemed as vast as all space and as enduring as eternity itself. It's true the sea is an uncertain element but no sailor remembers this in the presence of its bewitching power any more than a lover ever thinks of the proverbial inconstancy of women'' (pp. 287-88). The vocabulary, diction, and tone in this passage contain Conrad's meaning. Here we find references to *eternity*, *love*, and *betwitching power*—the words are abstract and metaphysical, and the cadences are musical. The sea itself, with its vastness, its beauty, and its might, Conrad tells us, encourages any sensitive person to reflect. Powell's final thoughts of woman and love exemplify his natural tendency to avoid pettiness and greed.

And love is an important part of *Chance*, albeit a very particular kind of love. To understand it we must understand exactly what attracts Captain Anthony to Flora De Barral. How can a mature, confirmed bachelor be attracted to a half-crazy and suicidal girl? They are both, in a heightened and quintessential sense, sea people, and this is what draws them together so irrevocably, despite the name of "Flora." Let us start by looking at Flora's entrance in the novel, when Marlow first becomes aware of her on one of his visits to the Fynes: "One day he saw a woman walking about on the edge of a high quarry, which rose a sheer hundred feet, at least, from the road winding up the hill out of which it had been excavated. He shouted warningly to her from below where he happened to be passing. She was really in considerable danger. At the sound of his voice she started back and retreated out of his sight amongst some young scotch firs growing near the very brink of the precipice" (p. 43). We find out later that Flora had been attempting suicide at this point. This passage also places Marlow in the role of the rescuer, a type that Conrad often portrays. Flora's first appearance in the novel suggests a painful awareness of suffering and realities like life and death. In fact, the attraction to suicide is one of the most dominant aspects of her personality and she often thinks of it as a relief from her terrible past and bleak future. As Marlow says: "Had she given occasion for a coroner's inquest the verdict would have been suicide, with the implication of unhappy love . . . . She retorted that, once one was dead, what horrid people thought of one did not matter. It was said with infinite contempt; but something like a suppressed quaver in the voice made me look at her again. I perceived then that her thick eyelashes were wet" (p. 45). Later in the novel, when Fyne is relating her past, he reports that while she was living with her cousins she sometimes escaped to the Fynes and on one occasion, rather than return, she threatened suicide. Suicide is mentioned again when she returns to England after her disastrous assignment as governess with the German family in Hamburg. Her troubles with her father, especially when he first gets out of prison and refuses to join her and Captain Anthony on board the *Ferndale*, make her again think of suicide: "'If he bolts away,' she thought, 'then I shall know that I am of no account indeed! That no one loves me, that words and actions and protestations and everything in the world is false—and I shall jump into the dock. *That* at least won't lie'" (p. 370). At many crucial points in her life Flora looks to death for an escape.

Flora's suffering is paralleled by that of her husband, Captain Anthony. The first description we have of him is through the rather obtuse "little Fyne": "Captain Anthony ('the son of the poet—you know') was of a retiring disposition, shy with strangers, unused to society, and very much devoted to his calling, Fyne explained . . . . He had had a rather unhappy boyhood; and it made him a silent man" (p. 46). The unhappy aspects of his past, especially with his father, connect handily with Flora's own horrible childhood experiences. That this passage appears within a page of Flora's attempted suicide solidifies their bond in the reader's mind. Moreover, when Fyne goes to London to talk to Anthony and try to stop the marriage, he finds him drafting a will—strange behavior for a bridegroom. He thinks of death even when he is in love. The combination of love and death is usually connected with Wagnerian opera in the Edwardian period. Marlow also relates that at the height of Captain Anthony's troubles with his father-in-law his thoughts would turn to death: "It would occur to Anthony at the end of such meditations that death was not an unfriendly visitor after all" (p. 397). Captain Anthony, like Flora, becomes suicidal on several occasions, which creates a strong bond between them. That both of them love the sea is part of this bond. Captain Anthony has lived most of his adult life upon the sea and although Flora had never had much contact with it before she met Anthony, her grandfather was a seaman. As Flora reminisces with Marlow at the end of the book: "I loved and I was loved, untroubled, at peace, without remorse, without fear. All the world, all life was transformed for me. And how much I have seen . . . . The sea itself! . . . You are a sailor. You have lived your life on it. But do you know how beautiful it is, how strong, how charming, how friendly, how mighty?" (pp. 444-45). Flora's happy life with her husband, especially after her father's death, immediately reminds her of the sea. The prose itself has a rhythmic cadence. The ocean pervades not only the second part of the novel but her remembrance of Anthony's love, and through her memory of his love he still exists to occupy her thoughts.

Much of this closely parallels many events in Wagner's *Der Fliegende Holländer*. Before the Dutchman and Senta fall in love they are desperately unhappy people, unhappy to the point of being suicidal. In the Dutchman's first monologue, quite early in the opera, he says:

> Wie oft in Meeres tiefsten Schlund
> stürzt' ich voll Sehnsucht mich hinab:
> doch ach' den Tod, ich fand ihn nicht!
> da, wo der Schiffe furchbar Grab,
> trieb main Schiff ich zum Klippengrunde,
> doch ach! mein Grab, es schloss sich nicht!
>
> How often into the sea's deepest throat
> have I longingly hurled myself,
> but death, oh, I found it not!
> There, in the awful tomb of ships,
> I drove mine on to the rocks
> but alas, no tomb enclosed me.

The music he sings to these words, with undulating rhythms that suggest the movement of the sea, is used for only two characters in the opera: Vanderdecken and Senta. His curse of solitary wandering has driven him to seek death, but the curse denies him even this relief; he must wander till he can find the true love of a faithful woman. Senta is supposed to marry Erik, a hunter, but her music suggests the Dutchman's wavy sea cadences. Her own loneliness is suggested by the sad ballad she sings when she first appears in the opera. She immediately sympathizes with the Dutchman's suffering and promises to be true to him unto death. She is exactly that at the end of the opera, despite her father's and Erik's attempts to stop her. Thus the Dutchman's curse is ended and they are both redeemed through love. The theme of salvation through love is basic to *Chance* as well as to *Der Fliegende Holländer*.

We must now examine Wagner's music to find a parallel to Conrad's sea symbolism in *Chance*. Water, which we have seen Conrad use so frequently in the novel, is used in Wagner here in the music rather than the libretto. An undulating, watery sound consistently surrounds the music of the Dutchman, his ship, and crew:

The recurrent crescendi and diminuendi in the strings create an effect that forcefully suggests the motion of the sea, and Senta's music has the same wavy rhythms. It is unlike the kind of music, light and often highly reminiscent of comic opera, that characterizes the other persons in the opera. In the second scene, after the other girls sing a merry spinning song, Senta sings her sad ballad:

Her voice, like the Dutchman's, is supported by the same undulating figurations in the strings; Wagner thereby connects her with the sea, and, by implication, with the Dutchman and death. By the end of the opera they are both dead, but redeemed through love.

The combination of love, the sea, and death, and the particular nature of the combination, which occurs in both the novel and the opera, have led me to suggest that the opera is a source for the novel. But what does Wagner's opera do for the novel? What is the purpose of the connection? We remember that central to Conrad's aesthetic of the novel is the idea of suggestiveness, a concept he absorbed from the French Symbolists. Wagner's opera has provided him with another dimension of suggestiveness, a musical dimension. We also know that Conrad valued music above all the arts. What this does for *Chance* specifically is make it reverberate with mythic and musical meanings that it would otherwise lack. We have already noticed the rhythmic, musical quality of many of the novel's descriptions of the sea; but these passages also suggest solitude, eternity, and death. The Wagnerian patterns also help to raise the novel above the sad story of two peculiar people onto the mythic level of an old and beautiful sea legend of love, death, and redemption.

With *Victory* (1915) Joseph Conrad once again used Wagnerian patterns to help create a suggestively operatic atmosphere. The love of Axel Heyst and Lena is similar to that of Tristan and Isolde. A prime factor in the comparison is the character of Axel Heyst, who is Tristan-like in his gloomy and cynical approach to life. Conrad motivates this gloominess by emphasizing the influence of Heyst's father upon the young Axel. The brooding skepticism of the father had a tremendous and unfortunate effect upon the boy. Conrad describes the father in the following passage: "For more than sixty years he had dragged on this painful earth of ours the most weary, the most uneasy soul that civilisation had ever fashioned to its ends of disillusion and regret. One could not refuse him a measure of greatness, for he was unhappy in a way unknown to mediocre souls . . . . Three years of such companionship at that plastic and impressionable age were bound to leave in the boy a profound mistrust of life. The young man learned to reflect, which is a destructive process, a reckoning of the cost."[22] Such a paternal influence incapacitated the boy in a subtle but profound way because Axel developed a passive, mere observer's approach to life, which fears and expects destruction at any point. The following passage in the novel dramatizes the father's final influence on the boy: "'Look on—make no sound,' were the last words of the man who spent his life in blowing blasts upon a terrible trumpet which had filled heaven and earth with ruins, while mankind went on its way unheeding" (p. 175). "Look on—make no sound" becomes a central principle in the son's life, and whenever he does not heed this warning, as when he runs off with Lena, he fears the results. The ominous presence of the portrait of the elder Heyst in his son's house warns the reader of the father's continued influence.

Wagner's Tristan is also very pessimistic, to the point of having a pronounced death-wish. During the *Liebesnacht* in the second act he tells Isolde:

> Stürb' ich nun ihr, der so gern ich sterbe,
> wie könnte die Liebe mit mir sterben,
> die ewig lobende mit mir enden?
> Doch stürbe nie seine Liebe
> wie stürbe dann Tristan seiner Liebe?
> . . . . . . . . . . . . . . . . . . . . . . . . . . . . . .
> Was stürbe dem Tod, als was uns stört,
> was Tristan wehrt, Isolde immer zu lieben,
> ewig ihr nur zu leben?
>
> Were I now to die, who would so gladly die,
> how could love die with me,
> the eternal die with me?
> So, if his love could never perish,
> how could Tristan die in his love?
> . . . . . . . . . . . . . . . . . . . . . . . . . . . . . .
> What could death destroy but what impedes us,
> that hinders Tristan from loving Isolde
> forever, and living but for her?

Tristan's strangely neurotic yet strangely attractive idea of love and death also occurs in *Victory*, for Axel Heyst also has a death-wish. His actions are very hard to explain unless this factor can be used to motivate them. He tells Lena, when he has discovered that he no longer has his revolver: "Here I am on a Shadow inhabited by Shades. How helpless a man is against the Shades! How is one to intimidate, persuade, resist, assert oneself against them? I have lost all belief in realities . . . . Lena, give me your hand" (p. 350). He transforms his enemies from three ruffians into metaphysical abstractions, but his feeling of helplessness is not the only possible response to the situation. Lena's reaction to Ricardo's assault indicates that she is capable of action, and effective action, in the face of mortal danger, though poor Heyst immediately gives up. He seems to welcome the threat of Jones, Ricardo, and Pedro. What but the death-wish could explain this kind of behavior?

Heyst is a fatalist who feels that he can do nothing in the face of brute force. As he tells Lena after they go to Wang's hut: " 'We are the slaves of this infernal surprise which has been sprung on us by—shall I say fate? your fate, or mine!' It was the man who had broken the silence, but it was the woman who led the way" (p. 353). Conrad cleverly dramatizes the contrast between the two. While Heyst philosophizes about fate and apparently wants to run to meet it, Lena still sees the possibility of escape and takes the lead. Several pages later the narrator says of Heyst: "He considered himself a dead man already, yet forced to pretend that he was alive for her sake, for her defence" (p. 354). But we know that not everybody on the island saw the situation as fated and hopeless; Lena certainly did not. When Heyst goes to confront Jones he says: "Are you trying to frighten yourself? . . . You don't seem to have quite enough plunk for your business. Why don't you do it at once?" (p. 383). This is neither the speech nor the action of a man who wants to live. Later in the novel the narrator comments: "At this moment, by simply shouldering Mr. Jones, he [Heyst] could have thrown him down and put himself by a couple of leaps beyond the certain aim of the revolver; but he did not even think of that. His very will seemed dead of weariness. He moved automatically, his head low, like a prisoner captured by the evil power of a masquerading skeleton out of a grave. Mr. Jones took charge of the direction'' (pp. 390-91). Heyst's death-wish is operating and Conrad again dramatizes it through contrast. Jones's evil but life-asserting action exemplifies thoughtless but efficacious behavior. However, Heyst, like Wagner's Tristan, assumes that the nature of life is inimical to his love, happiness, and very existence.

The death of Lena and Heyst's suicide are distinctly Wagnerian because of the love/death theme, and their ending even includes an immolation scene like the finale of the *Ring*. Redemption through love is clearly what is intended by the victory that Conrad claims for Lena. Some critics have suggested that this is intended ironically, given the deaths involved, but the theme is there in any case. Let us look more closely at Lena's death: ''Over Samburan the thunder had ceased to growl at last, and the world of material forms shuddered no more under the emerging stars. The spirit of the girl which was passing away from under them clung to her triumph, convinced of the reality of her victory over death . . . . Exulting, she saw herself extended on the bed, in a black dress, and profoundly at peace; while, stooping over her with a kindly, playful smile, he was ready to lift her up in his firm arms and take her into the sanctuary of his innermost heart—for ever! The flush of rapture flooding her whole being broke out in a smile of innocent, girlish happiness; and with that divine radiance on her lips she breathed her last, triumphant, seeking for his glance in the shades of death'' (pp. 406-7). There is a ritualistic, staged quality about this scene, an effect heightened by lighting, costuming, and the lyrically musical qualities of the prose—an effect like the ending of one of Wagner's operas. The sentences tend to be long and periodic, with abstract phrases like ''victory over death,'' ''profoundly at peace,'' ''flush of rapture,'' and ''shades of death.'' Lena's black dress and prone position imply that she is the victim in a fatal ritual. Her death, preceded by thunder and lightning but occurring in an exalted silence, is hardly realistic. The effect that Conrad has created is staged, operatic, and specifically Wagnerian. As in the *Liebestod* and the end of *Tristan*, love and death are connected by redemption through love. Isolde's final vision during the *Liebestod* contains her Tristan, beautiful and alive and loving her, and Lena's final vision in this passage includes the same elements of victory over death through love.

Let us now look at how Conrad describes the immolation of the lovers at the end of the book: "'I suppose you are certain that Baron Heyst is dead?' 'He is—ashes, your Excellency,' said Davidson, wheeling a little; 'he and the girl together. I suppose he couldn't stand his thoughts before her dead body—and fire purifies everything'" (p. 410). Davidson's suggestion of purification through fire and death is perceptive; Heyst's suicide, like Tristan's, is an attempt to become joined with the beloved. Just as Tristan thinks that his love can be fulfilled only in death, Heyst seems to be attempting the same kind of ultimate union. The fact of an immolation at the end is itself Wagnerian, although from the *Ring* rather than *Tristan*. But what is significantly different about this passage, when contrasted with the scene of Lena's death, is the obtrusive presence of Davidson. Here the quality of the prose is completely different and the effect is conversational rather than heightened and operatic. The love story is operatic in its situation and treatment, but the narrator brings us back to reality. Davidson's final comment, "Nothing," is all the real world can say in the face of the kind of love that Conrad, and Wagner, have portrayed.

A possible literary intermediary for the connection between Conrad and Wagner in this novel is hinted at by Heyst's first name, Axel. *Axël* is the name of a famous symbolist play by Philippe August Villiers de l'Isle-Adam. In 1869 Villiers visited Wagner in Lucerne and soon developed a passion for his operas, and this is reflected in *Axël*. The translator, June Guicharnaud, comments on the Wagnerian elements in the play in the follow passage: "The gold echoes that of the *Ring*, and the final *Liebestod* that of *Tristan und Isolde*. Even the form has certain characteristics of the Wagnerian drama, indicating a violent reaction to the well-made play and to naturalist literature in general."[23] Katharine Gatch has suggested that Villiers's play is the source for Heyst's first name and has also pointed out several similarities between the two works.[24] The extensive Wagnerism of *Axël* is certainly similar to *Victory*'s Wagnerian characterizations, situations, and imagery.

Though Conrad rarely mentions Wagner in his fiction, we have seen that he certainly uses Wagnerian patterns in a subtle and effective way. Some of Conrad's friends, especially Ford Madox Ford, were well aware of the German composer. A result is the use of Wagnerian patterns in some of Conrad's most important works. We have also seen that his theory of the novel drew upon the aesthetics of the French Symbolists, in particular their concept of *suggestiveness*. To create this suggestiveness Conrad sometimes drew upon Wagner's operas—specifically *Tristan und Isolde*, the *Ring, Parsifal*, and *Der Fliegende Holländer*. Like Wagner, Conrad was interested in myth and its potential for exposing the recurrent problems of mankind. Concepts like the death-wish, the power of money, the might of the sea, the curse of loneliness, redemption through love, and human determinism and images like the magic garden, incorruptible but corrupting metal, moving water, and purifying fire are common to both Wagner and Conrad. We have also seen from Conrad's correspondence and especially from the preface to *The Nigger of the "Narcissus"* how highly he valued music for its eminently suggestive qualities. Wagnerian music helped him to create a musical dimension in his own fiction, and the quality of some of his prose reflects this. Except for "Freya of the Seven Isles," where Wagner is mentioned in the text, it is impossible to prove that the rhythms in some of Conrad's prose are specifically Wagnerian, but they certainly are musical and their combination with the Wagnerian patterns we have noticed does create an operatic, staged, and mythic atmosphere. We have also seen that Conrad often used a nonparticipating narrator's lighter tone for contrast, which both heightens and balances the mythic effect. Wagner's operas provided Conrad with many examples of the union of music and myth, and thereby helped him give his own fiction "the magic suggestiveness of music."

## Notes

1. As reported by Donald Yelton in his *Mimesis and Metaphor: An Inquiry into the Genesis and Scope of Conrad's Symbolic Imagery* (The Hague, 1967), p. 54.

2. René Rapìn, ed., *Lettres de Joseph Conrad à Marguerite Poradowska* (Geneva, 1966), p. 132.

3. William Blackburn, ed., *Letters to William Blackwood and David S. Meldrum* (Durham, N.C., 1958), p. 155.

4. Paul L. Wiley, *Conrad's Measure of Man* (Madison, Wis., 1954), p. 14.

5. Bernard C. Meyer, *Joseph Conrad: A Psychoanalytic Biography* (Princeton, N.J., 1967), p. 145.

6. Ford Madox Ford, *Joseph Conrad: A Personal Remembrance* (Boston, 1924), p. 124.

7. Joseph Conrad, *The Nigger of the "Narcissus," A Tale of the Sea* (Garden City, N.Y., 1920), p. xiii.

8. Yelton, *Mimesis and Metaphor*, pp. 53-54.

9. See some of Wagner's essays for his high opinion of Greek drama, especially "Art and Revolution" and "The Artwork of the Future."

10. Joseph Conrad, *Almayer's Folly* (Garden City, N.Y., 1920), p. 208. Hereafter referred to in the text.

11. Wiley, pp. 34-35.

12. Joseph Conrad, *Tales of Unrest* (Garden City, N.Y., 1920), p. 236. Hereafter referred to in the text.

13. Wiley, p. 92.

14. Joseph Conrad, *Typhoon and Other Stories* (Garden City, N.Y., 1920), p. 236. Hereafter referred to in the text.

15. Wiley, p. 99.

16. Joseph Conrad, *Nostromo* (Garden City, N.Y., 1924), p. 52. Hereafter referred to in the text.

17. Winifred Lynskey, "The Role of the Silver in *Nostromo*," *Modern Fiction Studies* 1 (February 1955): 21.

18. E. M. W. Tillyard, *The Epic Strain in the English Novel* (Fair Lawn, N.J., 1958), p. 127.

19. Edward W. Said, *Joseph Conrad and the Fiction of Autobiography* (Cambridge, Mass., 1966), p. 158.

20. Joseph Conrad, *'Twixt Land and Sea* (Garden City, N.Y., 1924), p. 62. Hereafter referred to in the text.

21. Joseph Conrad, *Chance, A Tale in Two Parts* (Garden City, N.Y., 1921), p. 52. Hereafter referred to in the text.

22. Joseph Conrad, *Victory, An Island Tale* (Garden City, N.Y., 1921), pp. 91-92. Hereafter referred to in the text.

23. Philippe Auguste Villiers de l'Isle-Adam, *Axël*, translated by June Guicharnaud (Englewood Cliffs, N.J., 1970), pp. 197-98.

24. Katharine H. Gatch, "Conrad's Axel," *Studies in Philology* 48 (January 1951): 98-106.

# 2
# Situational Myths: Richard Wagner and D. H. Lawrence

Although we think of D. H. Lawrence as a thoroughly modern novelist who liked to shock the Victorians of his time, he was born in 1885. This means that his most intellectually formative years occurred during the Edwardian period. This chapter will show how and where he was influenced by one of the most dominant elements of the intellectual climate of that period, Wagnerism. In 1908 young Lawrence first left his Nottinghamshire village for a teaching assignment in the capital. Because Wagner was so much a part of the London artistic milieu at the time and because Lawrence wanted to become a part of that artistic community, he was naturally introduced to Wagner. The confrontation occurred, and influenced a great deal of Lawrence's early fiction; but it was more than simply the times that attracted him to the composer. Lawrence's interest in myth, at this time still primarily Christian myths, would naturally attract him to the great operatic myth maker. Wagner's desire to destroy his society's materialism through his operatic myths would have provided Lawrence with an early model of what he himself wanted to do, and would do later with Mexican and Indian myths, among others. Both artists saw themselves as living in a period of materialism, superficial values, and general decline, and both tried to renew their societes through their arts. Lawrence was interested in Wagner's operas because of the many similarities in their thinking, approach, and Messianic vision of art's purpose.

Some knowledge of Lawrence's early awareness of music and its place in his life would be useful. William Blissett's excellent essay on the novelist's historical connection with D'Annunzio and Wagner provides some background information: "With boyish impatience Lawrence gave up the piano after half an hour, but he encouraged his sister to play, could read music himself, and all his life he liked to sing. From the earliest days until the end, he and his friends used to sing ballads and folksongs together."[1] We can see from this that Lawrence did have a general knowledge of music, albeit an amateur's. His childhood interest in music was bound to blossom in London, given all the new musical activities available there. In Nottinghamshire the musical efforts were almost exculsively amateur, but in the capital there were many concerts, recitals, and operas at Covent Garden. This was the first time in his life that Lawrence could experience professional opera, and he did not miss his new opportunities.

One of the best sources for Lawrence's London period, his letters to Louise Burrows, did not appear in print until 1968. Lawrence met her during his years in Ilkeston from 1903 to 1905. That his letters to her have finally been published is especially important for my purposes, since they establish as fact that he was frequently going to the opera while he lived in London. Predictably, Lawrence's first reactions to Wagnerian opera were largely negative. Given his unfamiliarity with the works, to like one upon one hearing would indeed be rare. Since the music is complex and works slowly, it tends to need time and repeated exposure to make its effect. At the time one also had to contend with the Victorian productions available at Covent Garden, where attempts at strict realism in Wagnerian staging tended to have ludicrous results. These reasons may have combined to produce some of Lawrence's negative reactions. On 17 October 1909 he wrote to Miss Burrows: "I went to Wagners [*sic*] *Tristan und Isolde* last night, and was very disappointed . . . . *Tristan* is long, feeble, a bit hysterical, without force or grip. I was frankly sick of it."[2] Such a reaction is typical of a first hearing of the opera. Several months later, on 15 November 1911, he wrote to Miss Burrows: "On Monday I was up at Covent Garden to hear Siegfried—Wagner—one of the Ring cycle that I had not heard. It was good, but it did not make any terrific impression on me" (p. 149). *Siegfried* is an especially difficult opera. That Lawrence got some pleasure from a first viewing shows his perceptiveness. He became interested enough to see other parts of the *Ring*.

But perhaps Lawrence was seeing too much Wagner, for a nausea set in and he wrote to Miss Burrows on 1 April 1911: "I went to Cavalleria Rusticana & Pagliacci at Croydon last night—one shilling in the pit. It's an Italian company from Drury Lane—Italians of the common class—opera in Italian. But I loved the little folk. You never saw anything in your life more natural, naive, inartistic, & refreshing. It was just like our old charades. I love Italian opera—it's so reckless. Damn Wagner, & his bellowings at Fate & death . . . . If you were here tonight we'd go to Carmen, & hear those delicious little Italians love & weep" (pp. 88-89). This charming bit of exuberance is clearly a feeling of the moment, for he continued to go to Wagnerian opera and took it quite seriously. That the two operas he is extolling were put on by "those delicious little Italians" is clearly condescending, as is his remark that the final effect was fun but "inartistic."

In a more serious vein, Lawrence wrote to Blanche Jennings on 15 December 1908: "I love music. I have been to two or three fine orchestral concerts here. At one I heard Grieg's 'Peer Gynt'—it is very fascinating, if not profound. Surely you know Wagner's operas—*Tannhäuser* and *Lohengrin*. They will run a knowledge of music into your blood better than any criticism."[3] Lawrence's comment on Grieg's music is certainly perceptive, while the final sentence emphatically states his respect for Wagner's operas. Significantly, Wagner's music is connected with the theory of blood knowledge that Lawrence was beginning to formulate at this time. Eric Bentley has pointed out that during these years Lawrence reacted against liberalism, which placed humanity's greatness in its mental capacity.[4] By the beginning of World War I, Lawrence had fully developed his theory of the blood as the center of human perception, rather than the brain. That Wagner's music reaches the blood is, in Lawrentian terms, the ultimate compliment, implying that this music communicates with what is most essential and important in us.

Several years later, when Lawrence was living in Cornwall, he was often reminded of the Tristan myth. He wrote to a friend during this time: "I do like Cornwall, it is still something like King Arthur and Tristan. It has never taken the Anglo-Saxon civilization, the Anglo-Saxon sort of Christianity" (p. 409). In January 1916 he wrote to Catharine Carswell: "I like Cornwall very much. It is not England. It is bare and dark and elemental, Tristan's land. . . . It is old, Celtic, pre-Christian. Tristan and his boat, and his horn" (p. 413). Several days later Lawrence wrote to the Murrys that he still enjoyed Cornwall and still saw it in mythic terms: "The house is a big, low, grey, well-to-do farmplace, with all the windows looking . . . at a cove of the sea, where the waves are always coming in past jutty black rocks. It is a cove like Tristan sailed into, from Lyonesse—just the same" (p. 415). In these letters Lawrence constantly connected Cornwall with Tristan, and the land's mythic past clearly fascinated him. Although he enjoyed Italian opera, Wagnerian allusions appear in his correspondence. For Lawrence, Wagnerian operas were not immediately enjoyable the way Italian opera could be, but they tended to stay in his mind and appeared in his correspondence. The mythic dimension in the operas is probably what attracted Lawrence most, because, like Wagner, he was essentially and vitally interested in myth and its artistic possibilities.

Given the correspondence, the dates of the Wagnerian allusions in it, and the allusions in his fiction, one can date Lawrence's most intense interest in Wagner as between 1908 and 1918. It was during this ten-year period that he came under the sway of London and the capital city's current interest in the German composer. Lawrence's new acquaintances tended to be people like Helen Corke, Lady Cynthia Asquith, Bertrand Russell, and Philip and Ottoline Morell—people with musical as well as literary tastes—and for them, Wagner's operas were the avant-garde in music.

Emile Delavenay's biography, unlike the earlier one by Harry T. Moore, spends much time on Lawrence's formative development during his London years. Delavenay points out the Wagnerian elements in much of his artistic and intellectual development during these years. During his discussion of *The Trespasser*, he says: "Helen Corke and some of her musician friends probably revealed Wagner to Lawrence in the course of his rewarding London years. But the Wagnerian atmosphere may also be appropriately linked with the name of George Moore, particularly the Wagnerian evocations in *Evelyn Innes*."[5] Delavenay states that Lawrence also absorbed much Wagnerian thought through some of the nonfiction he was reading during these years. Houston S. Chamberlain greatly influenced Lawrence's thinking on race and aesthetics and from him he also absorbed a good deal of Wagnerism. Chamberlain lived in Bayreuth, married the composer's daughter, and wrote many essays on Wagner's ideas and music. Delavenay summarizes the connection between Lawrence and Chamberlain in the following passage: "The two men swim in the same romantic stream, that of post-Wagnerian aesthetics and Nietzschean anti-humanitarian mysticism."[6] Delavenay refers to the connection with Nietzsche again in his description of the Lawrentian aristocrat as "a Nietzschean and Wagnerian hero."[7] Delavenay also mentions Otto Weininger as a vehicle for Wagnerian themes. Weininger's *Geschlecht und Charakter* (1903) postulates a basic psychological difference between the sexes, which causes an inherent polarity of perceptions and functions. He also mentions Wagner in the book and describes the Wagnerian hero as masculine and Christian.[8] Much of Lawrence's early aesthetics and early fiction acquired Wagnerian themes, asserts Delavenay, through his reading of George Moore, Nietzche, Chamberlain, and Weininger—all of whom were much influenced by Wagner.

In addition to Emile Delavenay, Richard Aldington has also noticed the similarity between Lawrence's and Wagner's aesthetics. As Aldington has commented: "Long before Lawrence was born, Richard Wagner had written down the essence of Lawrence's beliefs and teaching.... Whether Lawrence had read Wagner's *Art-Work of the Future* or merely picked up ideas at second-hand cannot be determined, but everyone acquainted with Lawrence's work and life must see how he clung to them through all his many changes, waverings and self-contradictions."[9] Aldington finds several specific similarities in their respective theories of aesthetics, among them: art is at the source of life; art should bring unconscious, instinctive life principles to conscious awareness; and, art is not a production of the mind alone but of unconscious forces, which Lawrence like to call "blood knowledge." Wagner said that Beethoven's symphonies are great because of "an ordering principle so free and bold that we can but deem it more forcible than any logic, yet without the laws of logic entering into it in the slightest... it thrusts home with the most overwhelming conviction, and guides our feeling with such a sureness that the logic-mongering reason is completely routed and disarmed thereby."[10] Both Wagner and Lawrence also saw themselves living in materialistic ages with mercenary values and both men tried to save mankind through their arts. Wagner described most of the art produced in his own times in the following passage: "Its true essence is industry; its ethical aim, the gaining of gold; its aesthetic purpose, the entertainment of those whose time hangs heavily on their hands."[11] Wagner believed that man's materialism could be cured by a proper viewing and understanding of *Der Ring des Nibelungen*, and Lawrence's *Women in Love* tries to show that materialism is death-oriented and leads to loveless destruction. Both artists also used mythic vehicles to express their attempted salvation of their fellow-men. Wagner said of myth: "The incomparable thing about the *mythos* is that it is true for all time, and its content, how close soever its compression, is inexhaustible throughout the ages."[12] Lawrence's early years were steeped in Christian mythology and it, as well as Wagnerian mythology, is alluded to in his early fiction. Sex is at the core of both men's art as well. Wagnerian music is famous for its sensuality and its theme of redemption through women's love, while Lawrence is, of course, also famous for his view of the new life that love and sexuality can give man. But the greatest evidence of the connection between the two artists is to be found in Lawrence's fiction from 1908 to 1918.

Any discussion of Lawrence's early short stories is hampered by the problem of dates because it is often impossible to ascertain exactly when they were written since they were often published many years later. Warren Roberts, in his bibliography of Lawrence's works, gives the date when the stories were first published and tries to indicate when they were written, but he has to speculate on the early dates. Thus, with "Witch à la Mode" Roberts reports that it was first published in 1934, but written much earlier—probably before World War I.[13] Internal evidence also indicates that it is an early story and written during the period of Lawrence's Wagnerism.

The story involves a highly complex relationship between the two principal characters, Bernard and Winifred. The narrator comments early in the story: "Thus, after months of separation, they dove-tailed into the same love and hate."[14] An indication of the Wagnerian atmosphere is given by the music that Winifred plays: "When he came downstairs she was fingering the piano from the score of 'Walküre'" (p. 65). Bernard has doubts about seeing Winifred again right from the beginning of the story; he fears her. This fear is justified by her dangerous and peculiar personality, which is described several times as "witchlike." The situation becomes more Wagnerian because of its immolation ending, when Bernard runs away from her: "In another instant he was gone, running with burning-red hands held out blindly, down the street" (p. 70). Such an immolation, implies Lawrence, is the result of dealing with a neurotic woman in an ambivalent love/hate relationship, but while the fact of an immolation is only vaguely Wagnerian, the relationship itself is very similar to Tristan and Isolde's during the first act of the opera. There, too, a destructive combination of love and hate is dramatized and Isolde is portrayed as the evil sorceress who wants revenge on Tristan. She quickly decides to kill him, and herself, with a death potion, but her maid Brangaene substitutes the love potion instead. Isolde's intention to kill Tristan is a result of her intense hatred of him, but it is a hatred mixed with love. This is exactly the situation in "Witch à la Mode," and Bernard is almost burned to death by his witch. The Wagnerian elements in the story cleverly generalize the situation and relationship, and imply something about such human alliances. Although the characters themselves never become mythic, their situation does because of the Wagnerian patterns that Lawrence employs.

A peculiarly Wagnerian combination of love and death is at the core of "The Primrose Path." The story, first published in 1922, was probably written much earlier. The yearning for love is both psychologically and philosophically connected with the yearning for death by Wagner in his *Tristan und Isolde*, and Lawrence does the same thing on a much simpler level in this story. Matthew's hurried return to the Italian convent, where his dying wife had incarcerated herself, is futile. By the time he arrives she is already dead. The crucial passage in the story involves Matthew's reaction when the nuns bring him up to view his wife's corpse: "The three sisters flocked silent, yet fluttered and very feminine, in their volumes of silky black skirts, to the bedhead. The Mother Superior leaned, and with utmost delicacy lifted the veil of white lawn from the dead face. Matthew saw the dead, beautiful composure of his wife's face, and instantly, something leaped like laughter in the depths of him, he gave a little grunt, and an extraordinary smile came over his face" (p. 583). Though surrounded by three angels of death and covered with a veil, his wife's corpse reminds him of their former happiness when they were in love. Love becomes especially provocative in this atmosphere of death. Just such a peculiar ambiance of emotions is usually connected with Wagner during the Edwardian period.

Aside from the Wagnerian traces in these short stories, the first major product of Lawrence's Wagnerian phase is his novel *The Trespasser*. This novel is much neglected in the canon of Lawrence's work because the critics tend to dismiss it as either junk or juvenilia, or more commonly both. Certainly it is the weakest novel Lawrence ever wrote, but it is still, as such, deserving of serious critical treatment. It is typically Edwardian and certainly full of significant Wagnerian allusions, but Lawrence himself was rather ambivalent about the novel's worth. Although he allowed it to be published, he felt at the time that it was too personal and should have been given only to some close friends.

*The Trespasser* was first published in 1912, although Lawrence wrote it during the spring of 1910. There is much information in Emile Delavenay's biography for the factual basis of the work.[15] Helen Corke, one of Lawrence's teacher friends during his London years, had a traumatic love affair with a married man, which resulted in his suicide. Emotionally shattered by the experience, Miss Corke went to Lawrence for comfort and wrote of the experience as well. He tried to comfort her through the shock and read her memoirs of it; these became the basis for his own novel, *The Trespasser*. Helen Corke's version of the experience was published in 1913 as *Neutral Ground*, but it lacks the numerous Wagnerian allusions of Lawrence's novel. Thus we know that they are the product of his creative imagination and not borrowed from his source.

The Wagnerian allusions in the novel help Lawrence first of all to portray his two major characters. Early in the novel the following exchange occurs: "'What is it?' he [Siegmund] asked listening uneasily. Helena looked up at him, from pouring out the tea. His little anxious look of distress amused her. 'The noise, you mean? Merely the fog-horn, dear—not Wotan's wrath, nor Siegfried's dragon.'"[16] Later in the novel Helena compares a sunset on the Isle of Wight to "the Grail music in 'Lohengrin'" (p. 23). When Helena is at the piano, she is often playing Wagner. The rhythmic chugging of a train also reminds Siegmund of Wagnerian music: "The heavy train settled down to an easy, unbroken stroke, swinging like a greyhound over the level northwards. All the time Siegmund was mechanically thinking of the wellknown movement from the Valkyrie Ride, his whole self beating to the rhythm" (p. 189). After the lovers part and Helena goes to Cornwall, called by Siegmund "the land of Isolde" (p. 23), she is described there: "When Helena was really rested, she took great pleasure in Tintagel. In the first place, she found that the cove was exactly, almost identically the same as the Walhall scene in 'Walküre'; in the second place 'Tristan' was here, in the tragic country . . . . Helena for ever hummed fragments of 'Tristan.' As she stood on the rocks she sang, in her little, half-articulate way, bits of Isolde's love, bits of Tristan's anguish, to Siegmund" (p. 260). Toward the end of the novel the baying of two sheep dogs reminds her of Fasolt and Fafner, the two giants who built Walhalla in *Das Rheingold*. The final direct reference to Wagner occurs in a discussion between Helena and Cecil Byrne: "Byrne was thinking of the previous week. He had gone to Helena's home to read German with her as usual. She wanted to understand Wagner in his own language" (p. 290). Both Siegmund and Helena, in addition to Cecil Byrne, make repeated and direct allusions to Wagner and his operas. These allusions help to characterize Siegmund and Helena as highly musical people who are especially fond of Wagnerian opera. The music that they sing or hum also provides a musical atmosphere for the novel.

These Wagnerian references will also remind the knowing

reader of the Edwardian aesthetic novel, particularly as practiced by George Moore. His *Evelyn Innes*, the story of a great Wagnerian soprano, entails a detailed knowledge of Wagnerian music and production. The Italian novelist Gabriele D'Annunzio, also very popular in England at the time, liked the German composer very much. D'Annunzio's *The Flame of Life (Il Fuoco)* and *The Triumph of Death (Il Trionfo della Morte)* were rampantly Wagnerian in both allusions and generally fatal tone, particularly the Wagner of *Tristan*. Blissett reports that Lawrence enjoyed both these novelists during his London years.[17] B. J. Pace has emphasized Lawrence's reading of Thomas Mann's Wagnerian stories "Death in Venice," "The Blood of the Walsungs," and "Tristan" as another major connection with the composer.[18] *The Trespasser* is within an Edwardian tradition, but if name-dropping were the only reason for these references this would indeed be an incredibly dreary little novel. Because, however, the references are used for more important ends, the novel is still worth studying. They do much more than reflect Edwardian preoccupations with the composer, for Lawrence is using these apparently casual allusions as a method of characterization and to create a musical atmosphere in his prose.

The Wagnerian references in *The Trespasser* tend to fall into two basic clusters. The first of these centers around the opera *Tristan und Isolde*. Despite the fact that the hero of the novel is called Siegmund, his personality is closer to Wagner's Tristan. First of all, the death-wish is very much a part of his personality and this, of course, is the most famous aspect of Wagner's hero. Specific allusions to *Tristan* appear early. The sound of the fog-horn on the Isle of Wight frightens Siegmund because it reminds him of the horn calls in *Tristan und Isolde*. Helena says: "'It's something like the call of the horn across the sea to Tristan.' She hummed softly, then three times she sang the horn-call. Siegmund, with his face expressionless as a mark, sat staring out at the mist. The boom of the siren broke in upon them. To him, the sound was full of fatality" (pp. 26-27). Helena seems unaware of the full connotations of the motif she is humming. The melancholy English horn plays the shepherd's sad song to the fatally wounded Tristan at the beginning of Act III:

Right from the beginning the tune sounds a death knell for the lovers, and Siegmund is instantly aware of this suggestion while Helena innocently hums it. The fact that Helena is in Cornwall at the end of the novel fits into the pattern as well, since Cornwall is where the final tragedy of the opera occurs.

Siegmund's somber, death-oriented personality especially marks him as a Tristan-figure. Even when he is most happy with Helena, he thinks of death much as Tristan does. While Siegmund is in Helena's arms and they both seem happy, he says "death would wipe the sweat from me" (p. 164). Once he is back with his family his thoughts become even more suicidal: "'I can't endure this,' he said. 'If this is the case I had better be dead. To have no want, no desire—that is death, to begin with.' He rested awhile after this. The idea of death alone seemed entertaining" (p. 214). All this, of course, culminates in Siegmund's eventual suicide at the end of the novel. Wagner's Tristan attempts suicide at the end of each of the three acts of the opera, succeeding only at the end of the last, but Siegmund is immediately successful: "He was one shuddering turmoil. Yet he performed his purpose methodically and exactly. In every particular he was thorough, as if he were the servant of some stern will" (p. 251). Siegmund is indeed controlled by a sterner will than his own, for his death-wish has operated from early in the novel and the reader is fully prepared for the suicide when it finally occurs.

Death-wish and suicide also characterize the personality of Wagner's Tristan. As I have mentioned, he seeks death at the end of each of the acts and finally succeeds by ripping off his bandages at the end of Act III. Tristan says at that point:

O, diese Sonne! Ha, dieser Tag!
Ha, dieser Wonne, sonnigster Tag!
Jagendes Blut, jauchzender Mut!
Lust ohne Massen, freudiges Rasen!
Auf des Lagers Bann wie sie ertragen!
Wohlauf und daran, wo die Herzen schlagen!
Tristan der Held, in jubelnder Kraft,
hat sich vom Tod emporgerafft!
Mit blutender Wunde
bekämpft' ich einst Morolden.
Mit blutender Wunde
erjag' ich mit heut Isolden!
Heia, mein Blut! Lustig nun fliesse!
Die mir die Wunde auf ewig schliesse,
sie naht wie ein Held, sie naht mir zum Heil!
vergeh' die Welt meiner jauchzenden Eil'!

Oh, this sun! Oh, this day!
Oh, the bliss of the sunniest day!
Racing blood, jubilant courage!
Joy without measure, blissful madness!
How can I endure them, confined to this bed?
Then up and away to where hearts are beating!
Tristan the hero, in jubilant strength,
has snatched himself from death's grasp.
With a bleeding wound
I fought against Morold.
With a bleeding wound
I will capture Isolde!
Ha, my blood! Now flow joyfully!
She who will close my wound forever
comes to me like a hero, to save me.
Let the world go away as I hasten to her in joy!

The pattern of light and dark imagery in this passage is sustained throughout the opera. Tristan curses the sun as the enemy of his love but praises the night as its guardian. A conflict of light and darkness also operates in *The Trespasser*, though not in exactly the same way. Harry T. Moore comments briefly on this in connection with Helena's sunburnt arm: "There is a different kind of symbolism in the sunburn of Helena's arms, which is at one level a shrewd psychological presentation: Her arms become inflamed during the time she is with Siegmund on the island, and the burn lingers through the winter and into the following summer."[19] Aside from this, Helena's sunburn is also a part of a whole pattern of references to the sun. It is connected with the passionate aspects of love, while the gentler moon is used to suggest love's more spiritual qualities. Helena's sunburn suggests her inability to enjoy the sexual aspect of love. Hers is a lunar world, with its suggestions of the goddess of chastity. This sun/dark imagery suggests Wagner's *Tristan*, although Lawrence does not use it in exactly the same way.

Water figures prominently in both the novel and the opera. Act I of *Tristan* takes place on a ship going from Ireland to Cornwall, and while the lovers are on board they declare their love for each other. In Act III the wounded Tristan keeps looking out to sea for Isolde's ship; for renewed life and love he looks to the sea, but it brings him death. Such symbolical use of water also appears in *The Trespasser*. The following passage illustrates Helena's reactions to the sea around the Isle of Wight: "The rippling sunlight on the sea was the Rhine maidens spreading their bright hair to the sun. . . . The sea plays by itself, intent on its own game. Its aloofness, its self-sufficiency, are its great charm. The sea does not give and take, like the land and the sky. It has no traffic with the world. It spends its passions upon itself. Helena was something like the sea, self-sufficient and careless of the rest" (pp. 51-52). Obviously, the sea is an important part of Lawrence's method of characterizing Helena. Siegmund's response to the sea is described in the following passage: "He swam carefully. As he made for the archway, the shadows of the headland chilled the water. There, under water, clamouring in a throng at the base of the submerged walls, were sea-women with dark locks, and young sea-girls, with soft hair, vividly green, striving to climb up out of the darkness into the morning, their hair swirling in abandon. Siegmund was half afraid of their frantic efforts'' (p. 144). It is interesting that the sea reminds both of the characters of Wagner's Rhinemaidens, but their various responses to the sea are quite different. While Helena enjoys the cold, impersonal quality of the sea, it is this very quality that frightens Siegmund. He later gets an ugly cut when his arm brushes against a rock while he is swimming, an injury that parallels Helena's sunburn. Her enjoyment of the sea's impersonality implies something about her own impersonal nature. Siegmund fears the sea and its murky darkness and prefers the land and the sun. Wagner's *Tristan* also uses water symbolically, if not for precisely the same effect. There the water and its destructive powers unify the lovers, but in this novel it is used to separate them and imply that Siegmund is the truer Wagnerian.

Another cluster of allusions in the novel centers around *Die Walküre*. The most direct indication of this is the name ''Siegmund.'' It is interesting to remember that Lawrence's original title for the novel was ''The Saga of Siegmund,'' which emphasizes this even more. Wagner's Siegmund appears only in Acts I and II of *Die Walküre* and nowhere else in the *Ring*; but he is one of the most tragic figures in the whole tetralogy, for he is merely used by the gods, especially Wotan, in their greed for the ring. Like most of human beings in the tetralogy, Siegmund is fate-ridden; it is significant too that his motif, like that of most of the other human beings in the *Ring*, is in a minor key. His incestuous love for his sister Sieglinde is doomed to destruction from the beginning, while his death in Act II dramatizes his sad position as a mere pawn in the power plays of the gods in Walhalla. Is Lawrence's Siegmund also just a fly to the wanton gods? Certainly a tragic kind of fate seems to follow and finally destroy him.

The love of Siegmund and Sieglinde is surrounded by allusions to the moon. In fact, the moon is exclusively connected with these lovers in the *Ring*. They first discover each other's identity in the moonlight of Act I of *Die Walküre*. The point at which they declare their love is also when the moon begins to appear brightly, and by the end of the act Wagner's stage directions call for bright moonlight. Siegmund's famous Spring Song, mentioned in *The Trespasser*, uses moonlight in the following verse:

| | |
|---|---|
| Im lenzesmond | In the spring moon |
| leuchtest du hell; | you radiate brightly; |
| hehr umwebt dich | framed by your lovely |
| das Wellenhaar; | waving hair; |
| was mich berückt | what enchanted me |
| errat' ich nun leicht— | now I see clearly— |
| denn wonnig widen | for I delight my eyes |
| mein Blick. | rapturously. |

Moonlight also functions centrally in *The Trespasser*, primarily as a contrast to sunlight. We can see how the moon, as well as the sea, operates in the novel from the following passage: "Siegmund looked at her from his tranquility . . . . The cool, dark, watery sea called to her. She pushed back the curtain. The moon was wading deliciously through shallows of white cloud. Beyond the trees and the few houses was the great concave of darkness, the sea, and the moonlight . . . . 'I like the moon on the water,' she said" (pp. 43-44). This passage establishes a definite connection between Helena and the sea and moon; she is happy with the sea's lonely isolation and moon's chastity. The following passage also fits into this pattern: "In the midst of their passion of fear the moon rose. Siegmund started to see the rim appear ruddily beyond the sea. His struggling suddenly ceased, and he watched, spell-bound, the oval horn of fiery gold come up, resolve itself . . . . Turning to Helena, he found her face white and shining as the empty moon" (pp. 140-41). The moon, with its suggestion of chastity, is once again coupled with Helena and her fear of the sexual aspects of love. The moon, as well as the sea, is used by Lawrence to portray Helena's coldness and fear of sexuality. As in *Die Walküre*, the moon is used symbolically throughout the novel, though not for precisely the same effects. In the opera it does not suggest chastity.

Aside from symbolical similarities, the novel also mentions the opera specifically, as in the following passage: "Siegmund was there. Surely he could help? He would rekindle her. But he was straying ahead, carelessly whistling the Spring song from Die Walküre . . . . Was that the Siegmund whose touch was keen with bliss for her, whose face was a panorama of passing God? She looked at him again. His radiance was gone, his aura had ceased" (p. 128). The Spring Song reminds Helena of the heroic Siegmund of that opera, and her own Siegmund pales in comparison. This reference also adds to the musical quality of the novel. The Spring Song begins:

Siegmund's beautiful love song adds a sad irony here, for Helena is beginning to have doubts about her lover. It is interesting to note that Lawrence's original name for her was Sieglinde, but he changed it, probably because she is not the perfect Wagnerite that Siegmund is.

One of the most famous musical pieces from *Die Walküre* is the Magic Fire music at the end of the last act. It is during this part of the opera that Wotan kisses Brünnhilde, puts her into a magic sleep,[20] and then surrounds her with a magic fire to protect her from cowards. Only the hero who can penetrate this fire is worthy of Brünnhilde, and the fire will save her for such a man, eventually Siegfried. Magic Fire music also occurs in *The Trespasser*. When Siegmund is walking on the Isle of Wight, the scenery reminds him of the final scene of *Die Walküre*: "His surrounding seemed to belong to some state beyond ordinary experiences—some place in romance, perhaps, or among the hills where Brünhild lay sleeping in her large bright halo of fire" (p. 99). Such passages connect the novel with *Die Walküre* and its world of myth and doomed love. Siegmund is not just a married man having an adulterous affair, but a hero seeking his love. The situation is mythic rather than merely realistic because of the Wagnerian allusions.

One of the most distinguishing characteristics of the Wälsung lovers in *Die Walküre* is the fact that they are brother and sister. The incestuous nature of their love is emphasized by the goddess Fricka in the second act of the opera. She defends the rights of Hunding, Sieglinde's legal husband, against what she calls the perverted love of Siegmund and Sieglinde. According to John Stoll, along with Cavitch and several other critics, the relationship between the lovers in *The Trespasser* is also incestuous. Stoll has maintained that Helena is a mother-figure for Siegmund and that the relationship is like Paul Morel's obsessive mother love in *Sons and Lovers*. As John Stoll says: "The incest wish at the heart of the novel, . . . 'Eve-Mother,' establishes the reason for Siegmund's passivity, his increasing feminization, his infantile reduction, and his longing for death."[21] Stoll also quotes much of Siegmund and Helena's conversations and some of Siegmund's long monologues to her to prove this point. This incest is different from Wagner's opera, mother/son as opposed to brother/sister, but the element of incest exists in both works.

As we have seen, the Wagnerian allusions tend to fall into two distinct patterns that center around *Tristan und Isolde* and *Die Walküre*. *The Trespasser* is about a Tristan-like character with a marked death-wish, despite the name of Siegmund. The merger of love and death and the persistence of Siegmund's death-wish all point to a similarity to Tristan. A pattern of light and dark imagery, which in the novel suggests two different aspects of love, exists in both these works. Siegmund is happiest in the sun, with its suggestions of sexual love. The wound he gets while swimming is part of a series of water images that also connect with Wagner's *Tristan*. *Die Walküre* generates specific allusions to the moon, fire, and the incestuous nature of the love involved. Siegmund's surrogate mother, Helena, is consistently connected with water and the moon. She is wounded by the sun, balancing Siegmund's wound from the sea. But what good are these patterns of allusions? Lawrence uses them in the novel to elevate characters and situations to a mythic level. The Wagnerian allusions raise the elementary situation from a realistic albeit sad love story to the level of heroic lovers in a tragic conflict with tragic consequences. Evelyn Hinz has justly characterized the novel as: "a search for a material and form commensurate with an archetypal perspective and its inherent or mythological patterns—a mythos."[22] Lawrence also uses Wagnerian patterns as a method of characterization. Both Siegmund and Helena are sensitive and artistic people in the avant-garde of their period's musical taste. Helena's sorrow over the difference between Wagner's heroic Siegmund and her real and demanding Siegmund dramatizes her dissatisfaction with him because of his failure to attain the ideal and heroic. Finally, Lawrences's allusive use of Wagnerian symbolism adds a musical dimension to the novel. Wagner's sun, moon, and sea all connect with musical motifs and the lovers often hum various parts from the operas involved. In *D. H. Lawrence: The Croydon Years*, Helen Corke reports: "One evening this spring, D. H. L. brings me the first chapters of 'The Saga of Siegmund,' saying that there is the beginning of a work of art that must be a saga since it cannot be a symphony."[23] Lawrence was well aware of the musical effects of his novel. As we have seen, they often contribute the desired atmosphere of doom and fatality to *The Trespasser*.

We know from his later work that Lawrence did not remain the perfect Wagnerite who wrote *The Trespasser*. Even in this novel, his most obviously Wagnerian work, seeds of the future parting of the ways are suggested by its ending. When Siegmund decides to kill himself, he is certain that Helena, in orthodox Isolde fashion, will also kill herself: "She said she would come with—perhaps that is just as well. She will go to the sea. When she knows, the sea will take her. She must know . . . . She will come with me, he said to himself and his heart rose with elation" (pp. 247-48). But Helena does not kill herself at the end of the novel. Instead, she is in the midst of a new relationship with Cecil Byrne. She had been traumatized by her love affair with Siegmund and his subsequent death, but at the end of the novel she is slowly recovering and becoming attracted to Cecil. The novel concludes with the following exchange between them: "She laughed, and, making a small, moaning noise, as if of weariness and helplessness, she sank her head on his chest. He put down his cheek against hers. 'I want rest and warmth,' she said, in her dull tones. 'All right!' he murmured" (p. 292). Contrary to Siegmund's expectation, Helena recuperates from her experience with him and becomes involved with another man. Even in this most obviously Wagnerian of Lawrence's works, the life force is asserted at the end.

In the foreword to *Women In Love* Lawrence writes: "The novel was written in its first form in the Tyrol, 1913. It was altogether re-written and finished in Cornwall in 1917."[24] But, according to Moore, Lawrence's dates are not accurate; actually, the novel was finished in 1916.[25] The first draft was done within three years of his earlier Wagnerian novel. The German setting in the Tyrol perhaps worked its subtle influence on the novel, but in any case it does use Wagnerian allusions and uses them much more subtly and effectively than *The Trespasser*.[26] The Wagnerism of that novel has a *fin de siècle* quality that tends to date it. As R. E. Pritchard says: "Belonging to the time of the Romantic Decadence, as a young man he responded to the diabolism and sexual disturbance of Baudelaire and of Beardsley, the voluptuous synaesthesia and erotic mysticism of Wagner.''[27] Although Pritchard oversimplifies the Wagnerism of *The Trespasser*, the quality he describes is there. In *Women in Love*, however, the Wagnerian material is thoroughly integrated within the fabric of the novel and used much more independently. Lawrence was by then at the height of his literary powers and his use of Wagnerian patterns is tempered by his own genius rather than the period he happened to be living in.

Wagner's *Der Ring des Nibelungen* is most basically about the relationship between love and power. The ring itself, which will give infinite wealth and power to the person who possesses it, can achieve its power only if its bearer renounces love forever. Thus in the first scene of *Das Rheingold* the Nibelung dwarf Alberich loudly curses love when he steals the gold from the Rhinemaidens to form the ring. Of course it is partially their fault, for they tease him mercilessly when he tries to love them. His ugly body so repels them that they laugh at him when he tries to seduce them. This same dichotomy of love and power is at the center of Lawrence's *Women in Love*. Gerald and Gudrun, unlike Ursula and Rupert Birkin, are much interested in power and its uses, and it is this obsession of theirs that destroys their love and finally their whole capacity to love. Love, assert both Lawrence and Wagner, necessitates respect rather than manipulation and control. Wagnerian references thus surround Gerald and Gudrun although, as we will see, the whole tenor of the novel is Wagnerian.

The greatest number of Wagnerian references in *Women in Love* surround the characterization of Gerald. In the fourth chapter of the novel the Brangwen sisters are walking along a riverbank and see Gerald Crich swimming—this is when Gerald and Gudrun first meet. ''' He is waving,' said Ursula. 'Yes,' replied Gudrun. They watched him. He waved again, with a strange movement of recognition across the difference. 'Like a Nibelung,' laughed Ursula. Gudrun said nothing, only stood still looking over the water'' (p. 40). Ursula's laughing comparison of Gerald to a Nibelung begins a whole sequence of parallels. The

Nibelungen themselves are dwarfs who work in the bowels of the earth. In Wagner's version of the myth they had a happy and satisfied existence until one of their race, Alberich, robbed the Rhinegold from the Rhinemaidens (*Das Rheingold*, scene 1) and with the power it gave him enslaved his whole race, including his brother, to mine gold only for him. Alberich has renounced love for power and has made his fellow dwarfs, including his own brother Mime, miserable as a result of his thwarted sexuality. This is what happens to Gerald in the novel. He is owner and manager of the mines and his desire for efficiency and control over both man and nature incapacitates him for love, according to Lawrence's parable in *Women in Love*. He has even accidentally killed his brother, which Alberich does indirectly in the *Ring* (*Siegfried*, Act II). Gerald's power over his mines, like the tyrannical Nibelung's, is also fierce.

The miners in the novel are several times characterized as persons inhabiting another world, an underground world. Gudrun notices this immediately upon returning to the town after her long stay in London: "She could never tell why Beldover was so utterly different from London and the south, why one's feelings were different, why one seemed to live in another sphere. Now she realized that this was the world of powerful, underworld men who spent most of their time in the darkness. In their voices she could hear the voluptuous resonance of darkness, the strong, dangerous underworld, mindless, inhuman" (p. 108). Like their Wagnerian counterpart, the Nibelungs, Lawrence's miners really are a dark, separate race that has been enslaved by the force that dominates their lives and surroundings, Gerald Crich and his mines. They are no longer human beings, but "mindless" and "inhuman," and they are consistently connected with darkness.

How Gerald fits into this world is explained in chapter 17, "The Industrial Magnate." Gerald's attitude to the land and the coal is dramatically presented: "There it lay, inert matter, as it had always lain, since the beginning of time, subject to the will of man. The will of man was the determining factor. Man was the arch-god of earth . . . . What he wanted was the pure fulfillment of his own will in the struggle with the natural conditions'' (p. 216). Lawrence portrays Gerald's determination to control the earth in mythic terms with personified forces. His will to control is Wagner's power theme in another form, and there is something especially evil about it. His ''will'' tolerates no opposition to his desires. Lawrence makes Gerald's evil dominion over the mines dramatically forceful through contrast with his father's, whose approach was humanitarian. Thomas Crich ran the mines with a view to improving the lives of his men, but Gerald's new regime has a terrible and dehumanizing effect upon the miners. In *Das Rheingold* we hear frightful screams from the Nibelung dwarfs in scenes 3 and 4 because their lives have been terrified and enslaved by Alberich's new powers. Lawrence creates an equally somber picture in the following passage: ''As soon as Gerald entered the firm, the convulsion of death ran through the old system . . . . Terrible and inhuman were his examinations into every detail; there was no privacy he would spare, no old sentiment but he would turn it over. The old grey managers, the old grey clerks, the doddering old pensioners, he looked at them, and removed them as so much lumber . . . . He had no emotional qualms'' (p. 221). The ''convulsion of death'' also fits Wagner's treatment of the myth. In the fourth scene of *Das Rheingold* Wotan steals the ring from Alberich, which causes the furious dwarf to put a curse of doom and death upon anyone who owns it. As a result, death follows every owner of the ring as it does Gerald in this novel.

The miners themselves seem to have a strangely ambivalent reaction to Gerald's new power. Although they hate it in the beginning, they gradually swallow the propaganda that this is progress and the new Industrial Millenium. But: ''The joy went out of their lives, the hope seemed to perish as they became more and more mechanised . . . . They were exalted by belonging to this great and superhuman system which was beyond feeling or reason, something really godlike. Their hearts died within them, but their souls were satisfied.'' (p. 223) The insidious effect of Gerald's regime upon the men is here sadly apparent. Without their seeming to realize it, Lawrence tells us, the joy went out of their lives and their hearts were broken. Yet the miners somehow felt that there was something modern and mighty in their work and this satisfied them in a strange way.

One would think that Gerald would find satisfaction with the power and control he has gained, but his miners are not the only ones with broken hearts. Toward the end of ''The Industrial Magnate'' Gerald is portrayed as a very unhappy man: ''He would go on living, but the meaning would have collapsed out of him, his divine reason would be gone. In a strangely indifferent, sterile way, he was frightened. But he could not react even to the fear. It was as if his centres of feeling were drying up . . . . After a debauch with some desperate woman, he went on quite easy and forgetful . . . . He felt that his *mind* needed acute stimulations before he could be physically roused'' (p. 225). On this somber and menacing note the ''Industrial Magnate'' chapter ends. The mechanistic has replaced the naturally organic in Gerald's own sex life as well as in his mines. His mind needs sexual arousal for sex is no longer a natural, physical phenomenon for him. Gerald has unwittingly paid a very high price for his determination to mechanistically control the earth and the people around him; he has lost the natural ability to love. Like Wagner's Alberich, he has obtained absolute, godlike power at the loss of love. This is the meaning of the Nibelung reference when Gerald first appears to Gudrun. The curse of death is also operating in all the Crich funerals in the novel.

We can also see this curse functioning in the ''Death and Love'' chapter when Gerald kisses Gudrun as he is walking her home. The following passage recounts her thoughts while he is embracing her: ''So the colliers' lovers would stand with their backs to the walls, holding their sweethearts and kissing them as she was being kissed. Ah, but would their kisses be fine and powerful as the kisses of the firm-mouthed master?'' (p. 323). While Gerald is passionately embracing Gudrun, Lawrence reminds the reader that he is still part of the underworld kingdom of the mines. He comes to her not as a passionate man but as the master of the mines, the lord of the ring. Significantly, Lawrence reminds us of this when Gerald and Gudrun first approach love. The very title of the chapter, "Love and Death," hints of a Wagnerian meaning. When Gerald first makes love to Gudrun in this chapter, the fatal curse of the ring operates again: "Into her he poured all his pent-up darkness and corrosive death, and he was whole again. It was wonderful, marvellous, it was a miracle . . . . And she, subject, received him as a vessel filled with his bitter potion of death" (p. 337). Even in his love-making Gerald must reduce the beloved to his will; Gudrun is the subjected vessel who must receive the curse of death rather than life-giving sperm. While he can go into a peaceful sleep afterwards, she is neurotically awake and confused by the experience because she has been used in an ugly way, is vaguely aware of it, and resents it. Alberich's fatal curse has its Lawrentian counterpart in Gerald's inability to differentiate between love and power. His love-making, as a result, is suffused with "darkness and corrosive death."

I have traced the parallelism operating in *Women in Love* between Gerald Crich and Wagner's Alberich, yet there are other aspects in which the two characters clearly differ. For one thing Gerald, unlike Alberich, is handsome. His physical beauty, both facial and bodily, is repeatedly mentioned by Lawrence in his descriptions of him and various people's reactions to him. There is something definitely heroic about his stature as a beautiful male with absolute power. In fact, Lawrence occasionally uses heroic epithets to describe him. On page 210 of the novel he is called "Gerald, the gleaming" and on page 409 Gudrun calls him "my young hero." When Birkin looks at his corpse at the end of the novel he immediately thinks of an "Imperial Caesar." Certainly Gerald's heroic appearance implies a tremendous potential for greatness and goodness.

Lawrence presents Gerald's magical effect upon Gudrun

Brangwen early in the novel: "He was so beautiful in his male stillness and mystery. It was a certain pure effluence of maleness, like an aroma from his softly, firmly moulded contours, a certain rich perfection of his presence, that touched her with an ecstasy, a thrill of pure intoxication. She loved to look at him" (p. 169). The power of his beauty over Gudrun seems to transcend the merely human and realistic. Even while Gerald is desperately trying to save his sister's life in the "Water Party" chapter, Lawrence describes his intoxicating physical effect upon Gudrun. "Then he clambered into the boat. Oh, and the beauty of the subjection of his loins, white and dimly luminous as he climbed over the side of the boat, made her want to die, to die" (p. 173). The heroic dimensions of Gerald's characterization are consistent and mythically suggestive. He is more than beautiful; he is maleness personified, and Gudrun, we are told, is fated for him. The beauty has a mythic dimension that elevates him to a hero. Yet Gerald's beauty here too is mixed with an element of death, a touch of *Liebestod*.

Next to Gudrun, the person who most responds to Gerald's beauty is Rupert Birkin. This relationship builds slowly through the first half of the novel and climaxes in the "Gladiatorial" chapter when Birkin suggests a *Blutbruderschaft* oath between them. After Gerald refuses the offer, the relationship slowly disintegrates through the rest of the novel. On the last page Rupert and Ursula are talking about it and he mourns that it is over; it could have been, he says, a much better and healthier relationship. Let us look at the friendship at its peak in "Gladiatorial." Toward the end of that chapter, after the two men have wrestled, Birkin tells Gerald: "You have a northern kind of beauty, like light refracted from snow—and a beautiful, plastic form. Yes, that is there to enjoy as well. We should enjoy everything" (p. 265). Birkin's receptiveness to Gerald's beauty is here, at last, mentioned specifically. Gerald's northern good looks fit into the Wagnerian pattern, for his beauty is similar to Siegfried's in the *Ring*. The *Blutbruderschaft* oath that Birkin suggests is also within this analogy, for in Act I of *Götterdämmerung* Siegfried swears a blood brotherhood oath with Gunther. This parallel bolsters Gerald's position as Wagnerian hero and adds a heroic dimension to his relationship with Rupert.

Siegfried took the blood brotherhood oath with Gunther because Hagen gave him a drink that made him forget his true wife, Brünnhilde, and fall in love with Gunther's sister Gutrune. Gutrune is a false-Brünnhilde, the trap that ultimately lures Siegfried to his death. The relationship between Gutrune and Gudrun is parallel, for both women trap the hero and cause his death. Lawrence clearly went out of his way to use the name "Gudrun"—it is common in neither English nor German—to create this very connection with Wagner's Gutrune in *Götterdämmerung*. Harry T. Moore describes several possibilities for the source: "We remember that Gudrun is the name of Siegfried's wife in the Eddic version of the Siegfried story, and that the name Gerald is the old Teutonic word for spearbearer, warrior . . . . We cannot follow too far whatever Lawrence may have had in mind, but it is possible that he was using rather loosely the symbolism G. B. Shaw found implicit in Wagner's musical version of the myth, the symbolism of modern capital and industry. Certainly there is much about capital and industry in *Women in Love*."[28] Although Moore has trouble fitting together the hints from the novel into the old Germanic legends, they fit rather nicely in Wagner's version. Given this connection, Gudrun becomes the Gutrune of the *Ring*, the ersatz-Brünnhilde who is used to snare Siegfried into forgetfulness and death.

Moore also notices a mythic connection with the character Loerke: "This gnomish creature with full, mouse-like eyes seems to have much in common with Loki, the Evil One of Scandinavian mythology."[29] In Wagner's *Ring* this character becomes Loge, the god of fire and deceit. He appears in scenes 2, 3, and 4 of *Das Rheingold* and is always connected with trickery. When Wotan tries to get out of his legal contract with the builders of Walhalla, the giants Fasolt and Fafner, he immediately calls upon Loge to find him a way out. Loge's trickery parallels Loerke's, whose facile, industrial art manages to attract Gudrun. She eventually comes to prefer his company to Gerald's.

Moore also describes Gerald's death and its effect: "The mythological parallel faintly apparent in the story helps to produce an unusual suggestion of *Heldstod*, hero's death, that has an almost symphonic force . . . . Gerald goes up the high, snow-crusted mountain in the *Götterdämmerung* moonlight."[30] Moore notices here the Wagnerian suggestions that surround Gerald's death and make it much more moving. Gerald's implied connection with Siegfried elevates his death to epic proportions, or "symphonic force," as Moore puts it. Not only Gerald is dying, but a whole civilization. Moore's use of the term *Götterdämmerung moon* to describe the lighting during Gerald's death scene is appropriate, given the novel's final vision of England. Gerald's suicide, like Siegmund's in *The Trespasser*, is elevated to a mythic dimension because of the Wagnerian patterns used. A "Twilight of the Gods" is happening to English civilization as well as to Gerald by the end of the novel. Lawrence presents England as a land and a people destroyed by modern industrialism and doomed to a death of the soul and heart if not the body. This epic vision, with its picture of the destruction of whole races and civilizations, makes an analogy to Wagner's mighty finale to the *Ring* tetralogy apparent and even necessary. Few other artistic works have the scope and vision that could stand comparison with Lawrence's bleak vision of England in the finale of *Women in Love*. At the end of the novel Birkin and Ursula escape the darkness of northern industrialism and seek the sun of the south.

We have seen that two patterns of Wagnerian allusion surround the characterization of Gerald Crich. On one hand he is the master of the dark, underground world of the miners and in this respect he is Alberich-like. But this darkness is balanced by the "northern light" of his beauty and heroism and here he is like Siegfried. The darkness of the "Industrial Magnate" is contrasted with the lightness of "Gladiatorial" and "Death and Love." These conflicting image patterns symbolize the dual aspect of Gerald's personality, and they also match Wagner's use of light in the *Ring*. Alberich is consistently surrounded by darkness and it is usually murky or nighttime when he is onstage. Siegfried, on the other hand, is associated with sunlight and it is rarely dark when he is onstage. Lawrence uses these same lighting patterns to suggest two opposing aspects of Gerald's personality: the powerful miner and the beautiful but doomed hero.

In summary, most of the Wagnerian allusions in *Women in Love* surround the character of Gerald. They fall in two directions: toward the power-seeking Alberich and toward the beautiful and heroic Siegfried. Part of Gerald is monstrous and cruel and determined to control the lives of the miners and inflict his will upon them whatever the consequences, and in this respect he is clearly Alberich-like. But Gerald's beauty and heroic potential, plus the use of the Gutrune-figure in the person of Gudrun, create a connection with Wagner's fated Siegfried in *Die Götterdämmerung*; the blood brotherhood oath suggested by Birkin solidifies the connection. This pattern of allusions creates great poignancy during Gerald's death, for if he were only a grotesque dwarf the reader would be glad to have the bully dead. The heroic, Siegfried element in the character, however, makes the reader aware of the tremendous potential for greatness in him. Finally the entire novel, as a song of death for modern industrial civilization, especially in England, can be compared with *Götterdämmerung*. Both works portray the same situation of a whole society corrupted by greed and doomed to destruction.

What has Wagnerian opera done for Lawrence's fiction? The patterns of allusion do many things. First of all, they help make many of Lawrence's situations and characters heroic, mythic, and archetypal—this is true in "Witch à la Mode," "The Primrose Path," *The Trespasser*, and *Women in Love*. Lawrence was clearly dissatisfied with the realism in vogue during his time, and Wagnerian allusions helped him to create situations and characters that were mythic and heroic rather than merely realistic. The theme of love and death, and the connection between these two elemental phenomena, was one of Lawrence's central concerns, and Wagner's *Tristan* provided him with an artistic model for the theme. His "Primrose Path," *The Trespasser*, and *Women in Love* all employ this theme in different ways, while love and hate are dramatized in "Witch à la Mode." Finally, the whole scope of Wagner's *Ring*—its opposition of love and power, the results of the rejection of love, the theme of curse, and the destruction of a corrupted civilization—all become Lawrentian concerns in *Women in Love*. In that novel the Wagnerian patterns create a mythic situation that transcends mere realism, and here the librettos of the operas are the most important source of the effect. But in *The Trespasser* a musical atmosphere is created as well; Siegmund and Helena often sing or hum parts of the operas and thereby create a specifically Wagnerian dimension.

After *Women in Love* Lawrence's writings no longer display such a pronounced use of Wagnerian patterns, although some of the themes certainly remained. Thus, in *Aaron's Rod* the principal character is a professional musician and does play his flute during the novel, but never Wagner's music; there is a love-hate relationship in *Kangaroo* between Richard Somers and his wife; and love is combined with hate or death in "The Fox," "The Virgin and the Gypsy," and *Lady Chatterley's Lover*. But by the time of these works the themes had become purely Lawrentian and had lost their Wagnerian allusions and references.[31] Lawrence, then, went through a youthful phase of Wagnerism that produced several short stories, one good novel, and one great one, but after this he became solely his own man and artist.

It is interesting to note that toward the end of his life Lawrence came to think of Wagner's *Tristan und Isolde* as decadent and remarked that the opera "seems to me very near to pornography."[32] This is indeed quite a reversal for the man who wrote *The Trespasser*. Lawrence had learned from one of his earliest masters, gone beyond the experience, and could even dismiss him. Gratitude was not one of Lawrence's fortes.

## Notes

1. William Blissett, "D. H. Lawrence, D'Annunzio, Wagner," *Wisconsin Studies in Contemporary Literature* 7 (1966): 32.

2. James T. Boulton, ed., *Lawrence in Love: Letters to Louie Burrows* (Nottingham, 1968), p. 44. Hereafter referred to in the text.

3. D. H. Lawrence, *The Collected Letters of D. H. Lawrence* (London, 1962), p. 41. Hereafter referred to in the text.

4. Eric Bentley, *The Cult of the Superman* (London, 1947), pp. 228-30.

5. Emile Delavenay, *D. H. Lawrence: The Man and His Work* trans. Katherine Delavenay. (London, 1972), 1: 102.

6. Ibid., p. 303.

7. Ibid., p. 306.

8. Otto Weininger, *Geschlecht und Charakter* (Vienna, 1917), pp. 414-15.

9. Richard Aldington, *D. H. Lawrence: Portrait of a Genius But . . .* (New York, 1950), pp. 311-12.

10. Richard Wagner, *Richard Wagner's Prose Works*, trans. William Ashton Ellis (New York, 1966), 3: 318.

11. Ibid., 1: 42.

12. Ibid., 2: 191.

13. Warren Roberts, *A Bibliography of D. H. Lawrence* (London, 1963), p. 154.

14. D. H. Lawrence, *The Complete Short Stories* (New York, 1922), p. 61. Hereafter referred to in the text.

15. Delavenay, pp. 100-101.

16. D. H. Lawrence, *The Trespasser* (London, 1912), p. 26. Hereafter referred to in the text.

17. Blissett, pp. 22, 27.

18. Billy James Pace, "D. H. Lawrence's Use in His Novels of Germanic and Celtic Myth from the Music Dramas of Richard Wagner," Ph.D. diss., University of Arkansas, 1973, p. 10.

19. Harry T. Moore, *D. H. Lawrence: His Life and Work* (New York, 1951), p. 73.

20. On p. 411 of his biography of Lawrence, Moore briefly mentions what he calls the Sleeping Beauty motif in several of Lawrence's works. This involves a woman whose dormant sexuality is suddenly awakened by some male. Perhaps the sleeping Brünnhilde of *Die Walkure* is a source for this motif in Lawrence's fiction.

21. John E. Stoll, *The Novels of D. H. Lawrence: A Search for Integration* (Columbia, Mo., 1971), p. 55.

22. Evelyn J. Hinz, "*The Trespasser*: Lawrence's Wagnerian Tragedy and Divine Comedy," *D. H. Lawrence Review* 4 (Summer 1971): 140-41.

23. Helen Corke, *D. H. Lawrence: The Croydon Years* (Austin, Tex. 1965), p. 8.

24. D. H. Lawrence, *Women in Love* (New York, 1920), p. vii. Hereafter referred to in the text.

25. Harry T. Moore, *The Intelligent Heart, The Story of D. H. Lawrence* (New York, 1954), p. 174.

26. Since *Women in Love* and *The Rainbow* were originally conceived of as one larger novel, one would expect Wagnerian patterns in both of them. However, *The Rainbow*, a more old-fashioned generational novel, does not contain them. Perhaps Lawrence felt that the realism and final optimism of *The Rainbow* would be lessened by the mythic and darkened atmosphere that Wagnerian patterns give *Women in Love*.

27. R. E. Pritchard, *D. H. Lawrence: Body of Darkness* (London, 1971), p. 13.

28. Moore, *D. H. Lawrence: His Life and Work*, p. 139.

29. Ibid., p. 139.

30. Ibid., pp. 139-40.

31. B. J. Pace's fine dissertation also finds Wagnerian patterns in *The White Peacock, The Rainbow, Lady Chatterley's Lover*, and some of the shorter works. However, I find some of his assertions too speculative.

32. D. H. Lawrence, "Pornography and Obscenity," in *Sex, Literature, and Censorship* (New York, 1928), p. 68.

# 3
# Rhythm through Leitmotifs: Richard Wagner and E. M. Forster

E. M. Forster loved Wagner's operas all his life. He was moved by performances of the complete operas as well as orchestral excerpts at concerts, and for even more performances went to the Wagner Mecca at Bayreuth. What he especially enjoyed in Wagner's music was its specific definition and visual dimension. Forster liked knowing the literal and even verbal equivalent of the music he was hearing, and this of course is one of Wagner's fortes. As a result, he figures significantly in Forster's essay "Not Listening to Music": "With Wagner I always knew where I was; he never let the fancy roam; he ordained that one phrase should recall the ring, another the sword, another the blameless fool and so on; he was as precise in his indications as an oriental dancer. Since he is a great poet, that did not matter."[1] Wagner's leitmotifs are very useful not only for organizing music but also for giving the texts visual equivalents, and with opera, the text should be as important as the music. But Forster also recognizes the literary possibilities in this technique. In an interview with the *Paris Review*, he was asked:

"Do you have any Wagnerian leitmotif system to help you keep so many themes going at the same time?" Forster responded, "Yes, in a way, and I'm certainly interested in music and musical methods."[2]

Forster's *Aspects of the Novel* gives evidence of this interest and mentions music most in the chapter "Pattern and Rhythm." There he starts by discussing rhythm, "which may be defined as repetition plus variation, and which can be illustrated by examples. Now for the more difficult question. Is there any effect in novels comparable to the effect of the Fifth Symphony as a whole, where, when the orchestra stops, we hear something that has never actually been played? The opening movement, the andante, and the trio-scherzo-trio-finale-trio-finale that composes the third block, all enter the mind at once, and extend one another into a common entity. This common entity, this new thing, is the symphony as a whole, and it has been achieved mainly (though not entirely) by the relation between the three big blocks of sound which the orchestra has been playing. I am calling this relation 'rhythmic.' If the correct musical term is something else, that does not matter; what we have now to ask ourselves is whether there is any analogy to it in fiction. I cannot find any analogy. Yet there may be one; in music fiction is likely to find its nearest parallel."[3] Forster gets vague towards the end of this passage, partly because he cannot explain exactly what he understands instinctively, but rhythm is the phenomenon used to explain the unity of both symphony and novel. We will see that he uses this element in his own novels, and primarily through Wagner's leitmotific method, which helps him to create rhythm through the classic Wagnerian device of repetitions and variations of leitmotifs.

Wilfred Stone, while discussing Forster's tendency to kill off his characters quite suddenly in his early novels, says: "But though he tried to mend his ways in later books, those sudden deaths seemed right to him; they were part of his artistic vision. The characters must be able to come and go like phrases in a musical composition.

How else, save as rhythmic functions, can people live in an abstract world of art?"[4] Forster achieves this rhythm with Wagner's help; he saw structure as the essential difference between art and life, and a major way for art to communicate. Artifice is what gives the novel its ability to please—and its philosophic justification.

Forster's discussion about his own piano playing is indicative of his concern with the aesthetic principle of construction: " . . . and now to end with an important point; my own performances upon the piano. These grow worse yearly, but never will I give them up. For one thing, they compel me to attend—no wool-gathering or thinking myself clever here—and they drain off all non-musical matter. For another thing, they teach me a little about construction. I see what becomes of a phrase, how it is transformed or returned, sometimes bottom upward."[5] Though Forster is very modest about his own playing, the composer Benjamin Britten has said that "Forster knows his Beethoven sonatas (which I have heard him play with spirit)."[6] Significantly, Forster says that the primary reason he continues to play is for what it teaches him about construction. The variations and inversions of a musical phrase will find literary equivalents in his fiction, as we shall see.

Forster's profound interest in music is also mentioned in *Two Cheers for Democracy*: "Believing as I do that music is the deepest of the arts and deep beneath the arts, I venture to emphasize music in this brief survey of the *raison d'être* of criticism in the arts. I have no authority here. I am an amateur whose inadequacy will become all too obvious as he proceeds. Perhaps, though, you will remember in your charity that the word amateur implies love. I love music."[7] We also see the pervasive presence of music in Forster's thinking in some of his other essays. In "What I Believe," printed in 1939 when England was on the brink of World War II, Forster again has recourse to music, referring specifically to Wagner's *Ring* cycle. He is talking about the ugliness of strength, brute power, and Fascism: "The strong are so stupid. Consider their conduct for a moment in the Niebelung's Ring. The giants there have the guns, or in other words the gold; but they do nothing with it, they do not realise that they are all-powerful, with the result that the catastrophe is delayed and the castle of Walhalla, insecure but glorious, fronts the storms. Fafnir, coiled round his hoard, grumbles and grunts; we can hear him under Europe today; the leaves of the wood already tremble, and the Bird calls its warnings uselessly." [8] Comparing Fafnir with Hitler is brilliantly perceptive, and in fact earned Forster a position on a liquidation list that the Germans prepared for their planned invasion of England.

Wagner's operas usually combined a three-act drama with rhythmic repetitions of leitmotifs, through which he created his mythic operas. Except for the one-act *Rheingold*, the other three *Ring* operas are of three acts with interconnecting motifs. The major motifs are repeated with increasing force and meaning as the vast tetralogy progresses, and through them Wagner's meaning is subtly communicated. The corrupting powers of the gold, especially after it is formed into a ring, are made apparent through the strategic repetitions of the ring motif in all four of the *Ring* dramas. We hear it snarling in the orchestra in the third scene of *Das Rheingold* as Alberich enslaves all of Nibelheim to work for him alone. Wotan plots to capture the ring in *Die Walküre*, and here again the motif is repeated with the added force of accrued meaning. This motif is also heard in *Siegfried* when Mime, Alberich, and Wotan are plotting for it. When Siegfried gives the ring to Brünnhilde in the first act of *Die Götterdämmerung*, it has become a pledge of his love, but the audience immediately suspects what will happen to that love because of the ring's dangerous presence. We hear this motif again in *Die Götterdämmerung* as Alberich and Hagen again try to recapture the ring for their own evil purposes. Through repetitions strategic with the action onstage, Wagner uses his leitmotifs both to communicate meanings to his audience and to give his vast tetralogy rhythmic form.

My purpose here will be to discuss rhythmic form in Forster's novels, and not to catalogue all the leitmotifs in the novels. Other critics like Wilfred Stone, Alan Wilde, and J. B. Beer have done this already and very efficiently.[9] Rather, I will discuss the relationship between Forster's musical enthusiasms and his theory of the novel, and show how they operate together in his fiction to create a new kind of novel that is based directly on Wagnerian opera for its form. We will see his constructions as a literary equivalent for the Wagnerian device of nonrandom and varied repetition of leitmotifs to achieve form and commentary upon action, usually in a three-part construction.

But Forster's earliest uses of Wagner were much simpler than this. His first piece of fiction, a short story called "The Story of a Panic," mentions Wagner in passing. It appears in his anthology, *The Celestial Omnibus*, and all the stories involve some form of fantasy. When one of the characters in "The Story of a Panic" becomes rebellious, he is described this way: "He had stopped his running and was singing, first low, then loud—singing five finger exercises, scales, hymn tunes, scraps of Wagner—anything that came into his head."[10] The story is very simple and does not use leitmotifs, but the reference to Wagner and his music indicates that the composer was on Forster's mind and would reappear in his fiction, as indeed he does in the title story of this collection. Here Wagner is used much more significantly because of repeated references to the famous rainbow bridge that appears at the end of *Das Rheingold*. In "The Celestial Omnibus" the boy experiences the apparent fantasy of driving over a rainbow bridge in a celestial omnibus, but his father punishes him for being a liar. As the father tells his friend, Mr. Bons: "'Here is the great traveller! . . . Here is the young gentleman who drives in an omnibus over rainbows, while young ladies sing to him.' Pleased with his wit, he laughed. 'After all,' said Mr. Bons, smiling, 'there is something a little like it in Wagner'" (p. 63). But the skeptical Mr. Bons agrees to go for a ride with the boy on the alleged celestial omnibus, with the following fantastic results: "Yet, under his [the boy's] eyes, a rainbow formed, compounded not of sunlight and storm, but of moonlight and the spray of the river. The three horses put their feet upon it. He thought it the finest rainbow he had seen, but did not dare to say so, since Mr. Bons said that nothing was there. He leant out—the window had opened—and sang the tune that rose from the sleeping waters. 'The prelude to Rheingold?' said Mr. Bons suddenly. 'Who taught you these leitmotifs?' " (p. 71). The image of the rainbow bridge obsessed Forster for a long while, for it reappears in *Howards End*, where it becomes symbolical.

Forster's first use of Wagnerian construction appears in his first novel, *Where Angels Fear to Tread* (1905). The overall structure contrasts English values with Italian values. The latter are good and the former are bad, Philip Herriton is wont to say over and over again early in the novel, to irritate his mother and sister. Forster is wiser than this, and Philip will also become wiser by the end of the novel. In Italy there is antiquity, beauty, and emotional honesty, all of which are missing in England and especially in the suffocating upper-middle-class life of Sawston. But in Italy there is also a lack of honor and purpose, a general muddle, and severe repression of women. Those are the general rhythms, to use Forster's own terminology, and most of the characters are at one end or the other, but the more interesting, rounded characters hover around the middle. Mrs. Herriton and her grim daughter Harriet are chauvinistically English and stand firmly at that extreme, while Gina and Lilia are brainlessly Italianate and are glued there, and for Lilia this ultimately results in unhappiness and death. Caroline Abbot and Philip Herriton, however, learn by the end of the novel to combine English efficiency and purpose with Italian passion and emotional honesty.

The Wagnerian element in this novel is rhythmic structure, achieved through leitmotifs. In addition to the thematic ones discussed, Forster also uses repeated phrases for several reasons, but primarily for characterization. Thus he uses both theme and variation, the Wagnerian device that he had mentioned in his discussion of rhythm in the novel, in *Where Angels Fear to Tread*. An early example of such use occurs on the third page, when Harriet Herriton first appears. The scene is the railroad station as Lilia

Herriton and Caroline Abbott are about to leave for Italy. In the midst of the confusion and leave-taking: "'Handkerchiefs and collars,' screamed Harriet, 'in my inlaid box! I've lent you my inlaid box.'"[11] This inlaid box becomes a leitmotif to help the reader understand Harriet. It will recur repeatedly in the novel and become irrevocably identified with her. How does it help us to identify Harriet Herriton among the other minor characters and to understand her function in the whole pattern of the novel? An inlaid box is an object, an inorganic thing, uselessly decorative. It also suggests something enclosing, smothering, and part of the delicate accrual of the proper Victorian spinster. This is certainly how Harriet functions in the novel, for she mindlessly defends old nineteenth-century English concepts like Puritanical Christianity, Duty, and English Imperialism. That box is a useful way of remembering her. The pattern culminates in the opening of the eleventh chapter, right after she has caused the death of Lilia and Gino's child: "The details of Harriet's crime were never known. In her illness she spoke more of the inlaid box that she lent to Lilia—lent, not given—than of recent troubles" (p. 165). Here the box takes on more somber meanings, suggesting a coffin for the infant that Harriet, and all that she represents, has killed. The inlaid box has become a leitmotif that adds a sad, ironic touch to the death of the child, and suggests what really killed it. Like Wagner, Forster can use leitmotifs for added poignancy and irony.

One of Gino's major leitmotifs is his repeated spitting. This motif creates an interesting contrast with Harriet's, for his action is natural, organic, and lower-class Italian. It helps us both to identify Gino and to understand how Forster means us to see him—as wholly natural but a bit repulsive to a middle-class Englishman. Another Italian leitmotif appears later when Philip Herriton casually comments that the famous tower of Monteriano is a symbol of the town. Forster's source here is the famous towers of San Gemignano, the real Monteriano. The tower is repeatedly mentioned, and it finally becomes a symbol not only of the town but of all Italy. The phallic implications are obvious. Italy as the land of passion and fertility is clearly suggested by this motif and supported by the birth of Lilia's baby and Gino's children after that. In England no one seems to have children, at least not for the duration of this novel. The tower also suggests the ancient beauty of Italy, thereby connecting artistic beauty with passion and fertility. Again the repetition of the leitmotif gives rhythmic form to *Where Angels Fear to Tread*, through accrued meaning.

If form is meaning in *Where Angels Fear to Tread*, then Forster's form suggests a vision of life as a total pattern whose variations affect us significantly but impersonally. In such a world angels, indeed, would fear to tread. Clearly Forster's aim of rhythm in the novel has shaped the form of this book, and Wagner's influence is apparent and helpful. How can one give form to an episodic novel? This was Forster's problem and Wagner provided him with a solution. The end result is a novel with social meanings that are never stated in the novel, but appear through Forster's subtle uses of leitmotif. It is like what we hear just after Beethoven's Fifth Symphony has stopped.

In Forster's next novel, *The Longest Journey* (1907), all of the Wagnerian allusions are in the first part of the book, "Cambridge," and help to establish its intellectual setting. On the fourth page the first of these occurs: "The other philosophers were crouched in odd shapes on the sofa and table and chairs, and one, who was a little bored, had crawled to the piano and was timidly trying the Prelude to Rhinegold with his knee upon the soft pedal. The air was heavy with good tabacco-smoke and the pleasant warmth of tea, and as Rickie became more sleepy the events of the day seemed to float one by one before his acquiescent eyes."[12] In comfortable Cambridge Rickie, one of the student "philosophers," is quite content to snooze and listen to some Wagner. All this companionable comfort is destroyed by the entrance of Agnes Pembroke, which Rickie later described in accord with the music being played on the piano: "But she is really nice. And I thought she came into the room so beautifully. Do you know—oh, of course, you despise music—but Anderson was playing Wagner, and he's just got to the part where they sing 'Rheingold!' and the sun strikes into the waters, and the music, which up to then has so often been in E flat—'' (p. 17). Comparing Agnes Pembroke's entrance in the novel to one of the most beautiful moments of the *Ring* is certainly high praise, praise that will prove ironic very quickly. Later in the novel, when Rickie and Ansell are exchanging letters, Wagnerian heroines are mentioned in their correspondence. Ansell has written to Rickie to try to dissuade him from marrying Agnes, but Rickie answers that he is in love and wants to marry the girl: ''Understand Beatrice, and Clara Middleton, and Brunhilde in the first scene of Götterdämmerung'' (p. 89). Ansell's next letter warns: ''Understand Xanthippe, and Mrs. Bennet, and Elsa in the question scene of Lohengrin'' (p. 89). Rickie defends his position with the example of the loving Brünnhilde, while Ansell warns him with that of the doubting, destructive Elsa. Agnes turns out to be much more of an Elsa than a Brünnhilde, but only Ansell can see that at this point in the novel. Tristan and Isolde are also mentioned, when Rickie tells Agnes early in their courtship: ''I can't soar; I can only indicate. That's where the musicians have the pull, for music has wings, and when she says 'Tristan' and he says 'Isolde,' you are on the heights at once'' (p. 154). Forster's belief that music is the superior art form because of its greater capacity for subtlety is evident here. Interesting too is Rickie's recognition that, unlike Gerald and Stephen, he is an unheroic type who really cannot soar.

All the Wagnerian allusions in the novel occur in the ''Cambridge'' section, which thereby acquires a mythological and musical atmosphere. The next locale, Sawston, lacks both myth and music. Nevertheless, the problem of rhythm, as Forster saw it, has to be handled. For the novelist the problem is, how does one give form to an episodic novel? Merely moving from one episode to another struck Forster as sloppy art; he wanted a form that communicated a meaning. *The Longest Journey* is divided into three major sections—Cambridge, Sawston, and Wiltshire. Leitmotifs also occur in this novel—for example, the highly suggestive picture of Demeter that keeps appearing, as well as the head of Hermes. Both remind the reader of Greek mythology, which Rickie is so fond of, as of course was Forster; this is his most autobiographical book. Rickie's short stories, "Pan Pipes," which deal with the Greek deity Pan, keep getting mentioned in the novel. This recurrent motif of Greek mythology is significant in the novel for it helps describe the nature of a character. Greece, then, is a fourth location in the novel, and though there is no specific section named for it, its influence is manifest in all other parts of the book. In the Cambridge section, though, it is especially important, for Cambridge is the mythological place where Rickie might have been happy had he stuck to male companionship and avoided the trap of marriage. The similarities between Cambridge and Greece—for example, the prevalence of homosexuality—create dimensions of meaning in the character. Thus *The Longest Journey* uses leitmotifs more subtly than Forster's first novel, connecting locations as well as characters and ideas.

A pattern of circles occurs throughout the novel as well. The Cadbury Rings and the dell are rounded and suggest entrapment, for in the former, Aunt Emily tells Rickie of his bastard brother, and in the latter, Agnes ambushes him into a marriage. This creates another trap, symbolized by the ring of marriage on Rickie's finger. That one of the recurrent images is a ring is interesting, since Wagner, of course, is famous for his use of this image, but he uses it in a very different way, to suggest greed and power rather than confinement. Wilfred Stone's excellent chapter on this novel is aptly entitled "The Slaughter of the Innocents," for the lame, weak Rickie is indeed an innocent trapped by what he doesn't understand, and finally he is killed. What gives the ending of this novel greater poignancy is its rhythmic form. The motif of circles tells the reader early in the novel that Rickie is as doomed as were the Innocents before Herod's soldiers.

In Forster's lightest—he called it his "nicest"—novel, *A Room with a View* (1908), Wagner functions too. And although the use Forster makes of the composer here is not very profound, it is innovative, for in this novel allusions are comic. In the twelfth chapter, during the bathing scene, three men are described in mock Wagnerian terms: "Three gentlemen rotated in the pool breast high, after the fashion of the nymphs in 'Götterdämmerung.'"[13] To compare silly Freddy, ministerial Mr. Beebe, and aggressive George to the Rhinemaidens in the final *Ring* opera is laughably incongruous. This same kind of deflating comedy occurs again in the novel when Lucy tries to play some of the Flower Maidens' music from *Parsifal*. She plays the piece so badly that her brother Freddy suggests that they go and play tennis instead; she cheerfully agrees and closes the piano. Here too the reference to Wagner is used for comic effect, which is appropriate for Forster's happiest and sunniest novel.

Wilfred Stone briefly discusses the rhythms in this novel: "Medieval versus classical, ascetic versus pagan, and Gothic versus Greek—these are some of the important sets of contrasts that create the 'rhythm' of the novel. Along with truth versus lies, light versus darkness, and views versus rooms, these are the symbolic antitheses that make up the book's tapestry of interwoven themes."[14] All this is most perceptive, and Forster's subtle uses of these motifs are structurally Wagnerian. The highly ironic use of the motif of room is apparent in the following passage: "Of course Miss Bartlett accepted. And, equally of course, she felt sure that she would prove a nuisance, and begged to be given an inferior spare room—something with no view, anything" (p. 164). The concepts of view and room, both of which have major symbolic import in the novel, are played with here. The spinsterly Miss Bartlett is never capable of a view, and Forster suggests this here. As does *Where Angels Fear to Tread*, this novel contrasts Italy, the land of freedom and passion, with England's web of social conventions and suppressions. By the end of the novel the young lovers are in Italy again, and happily married. Most of these social themes had appeared in Forster's earlier novels, hence in a thematic sense this novel is not breaking new ground. For Forster the work was a pleasant entrenchment and happy reiteration of themes that were treated more seriously in his earlier two novels. As a result, this novel is his most comic, happy work, but it does not reverberate with the more serious, manifold meanings of his earlier ones. Wagner has not been used very profoundly here because the fabric Forster has woven is of simpler design. Perhaps Forster needed a rest after *The Longest Journey* and before approaching what would become his greatest novel and one of the masterpieces of English literature.

*Howards End* (1910), like all of Forster's earlier novels, is laced with Wagnerian allusions, which help to communicate particular meanings and to establish a specificially Edwardian intellectual milieu. Early in the novel Margaret talks heatedly about the confusing connections between the arts: "But, of course, the real villain is Wagner. He has done more than any man in the nineteenth century towards the muddling of the arts. I do feel that music is in a very serious state just now, though extraordinarily interesting. Every now and then in history there do come these terrible geniuses, like Wagner, who stir up all the wells of thought at once. For a moment it's splendid. Such a splash as never was. But afterwards—such a lot of mud; and the wells—as it were, they communicate with each other too easily now, and not one of them will run quite clean. That's what Wagner's done."[15] Margaret is perceptive here in recognizing Wagner's immense influence upon a succeeding generation of artists and thinkers. What she is specifically referring to is his theory of the *Gesamtkunstwerk*, the total art work that would include music, painting, drama, the dance, sculpture, and acting. Wagner felt that his own music-dramas, as he liked to call them, would tap all the other arts in order to produce his *Gesamtkunstwerk*. As Margaret points out, this muddied up the artistic waters and encouraged people to look at Monets and think of Debussy's music, or to hear his music and try to visualize Monet's paintings. A theory of total togetherness for the arts can become a confusion of the arts that Wagner never intended. Margaret's discussion indicates that she knows where the new directions in the arts are in her time, and what their sources are.

The opening of chapter 22, one of the most important passages in the book and clearly stating its major theme, uses an image derived from *Rheingold*: "Margaret greeted her lord with peculiar tenderness on the morrow. Mature as he was, she might yet be able to help him to the building of the rainbow bridge that should connect the prose in us with the passion. Without it we are meaningless fragments, half monks, half beasts; unconnected arches that have never joined into a man. With it love is born, and alights on the highest curve, glowing against the grey, sober against the fire. Happy the man who sees from either aspect the glory of these outspread wings. The roads of his soul lie clear, and he and his friends shall find easy going" (p. 186). The image of the rainbow bridge, which Forster has also used in "The Celestial Omnibus," appears here too to exemplify the concept of connection that is at the core of the novel. *Only connect*, the novel's epigraph, is also its central meaning. Reality and happiness do not exist at extremes, but through the connection of extremes. As Forster says farther down on the same page: "Only connect! That was the whole of her sermon. Only connect the prose and the passion, and both will be exalted, and human love will be seen at its height. Live in fragments no longer. Only connect, and the beast and the monk, robbed of the isolation that is life to either, will die" (pp. 186-87). The rainbow bridge that appears at the end of *Das Rheingold* connects the gods with their glorious new home, Walhalla. The beauty and usefulness of the rainbow bridge magically connect for a glorious finale in the opera. That same glorious finale, suggests Forster, is at the core of his novel through the concept of connection.

But Wagner's influence upon this novel is more pervasive and important than an occasional allusion to help with characterization and theme. *Howards End* is Forster's most Wagnerian novel because its use of leitmotifs is most complex and subtle. As Wilfred Stone has said: "To read this novel as Forster would have us read it, we must conceive of it as a kind of musical score in which leitmotifs associated with certain characters and situations are of special importance. And it is the alternation of these leitmotifs that provides what, essentially, Forster means by 'rhythm.' The book's rhythms are carried mainly by key phrases, and words within these phrases, which are stated and repeated in ever-widening circles of meanings."[16] The major motif of the novel appears on the title page: "Only connect." This central motif also appears in Margaret's dialogue in a very important scene in the novel, when she defends her pregnant sister against Henry's order that they leave Howards End: "'Not any more of this,' she cried. 'You shall see the connection if it kills you, Henry! You have had a mistress—I forgave you. My sister has a lover—you drive her from the house. Do you see the connection?'" (p. 308). But Henry doesn't, though Margaret presents it in all its ugly clarity. Henry can't connect, but Forster wants the reader to be able to, like the admirable characters in this book, especially Margaret and Ruth Wilcox. To connect is to see clearly and act decisively, to understand fully and behave accordingly, to see steadily and wholly, to bridge the gaps.

Another of the leitmotifs in the novel is hay and hay fever. Though the Wilcoxes are the technical owners of Howards End—symbolically England—they all get hay fever there except for Mrs. Wilcox, which suggests that they are not meant to be its final owners. But the Schlegels, except for the effeminate Tibby, do not get hay fever from the country and they enjoy it very much, which implies that they should own it, as they eventually do. Hay fever thus becomes a motif suggesting moral versus legal rights of ownership. In the *Ring*, only the race of the Wälsungs can wield the sword Nothung, and this ability comes to symbolize their paternal rights. Hay and hay fever operate in a similar manner and, through repetition and variation, Forster's concepts of accord with nature and moral ownership are communicated. He uses this motif ironically for Tibby Schlegel, whose hay fever reaches epic proportions and dramatizes his incapacity to either enjoy nature or rule England. Though this motif is minor in the novel, it is repeated nonrandomly and for decidedly rhythmic effect.

Wagner is famous for his characterization, both musically and dramatically, and the technique he uses most frequently is to give all his major and minor characters a leitmotif that characterizes them and that also helps the audience to remember them. Fasolt and Fafner, the two giants in *Rheingold*, are not Tweedle-Dum and Tweedle-Dee; they are distinguishable because of Wagner's subtle uses of leitmotifs. Also in *Rheingold*, Wotan, Fricka, Erda, Freia, Loge, Donner, and Alberich all have their own motifs. Forster similarly uses leitmotifs to differentiate his characters. For example, Leonard Bast's umbrella recurs throughout the opening of the novel and is a way of remembering him. The Schlegels take the umbrella from him by accident and he struggles to get it back, all of which is phallic symbolism. The conflicts over the disappearance of the umbrella suggest that the upper classes steal the masculinity and vitality of the lower classes, and by the end of the novel Helen does this by indirectly causing Leonard's death. The phrase *panic and emptiness* first occurs in the novel when Forster describes Helen's reaction to hearing Beethoven's Fifth Symphony, and the phrase dogs her throughout the novel. It is a clever way of differentiating her from her sister Margaret, who is much more stable, though much less attractive. Food is usually present whenever Tibby is around, and this motif often produces comedy. When Helen goes to his rooms at Oxford to talk about her personal problems and breaks down and weeps, Tibby is more concerned that his apple charlotte pudding will get cold.

Wagner often used motifs to comment upon the action of the drama. Thus, while Wotan is trying to decide whether or not to give the ring to the giants Fasolt and Fafner, the curse motif is heard in the orchestra. Wagner is telling us through his orchestra what will happen to Wotan if he does not give up the ring. Forster uses leitmotif ironically to achieve the same effect, as well as to communicate ideas. The phrase *telegrams and anger* is often used by Forster just when things are about to get ugly, a way of warning us of what will soon occur. *Odors from the abyss* recurs, to characterize how the wealthy Schlegels view Leonard's pathetic poverty. Howards End and the wych-elm next to it work together harmonically, like the male and female principles, and they are usually described together as a single, complementary unit. Like Wagner, Forster uses leitmotifs to communicate major ideas and themes, to help portray his characters, to achieve comic effect, and to comment upon the progression of the action.

In *A Passage to India* (1924), the main symbol of the Malabar Caves and the mystery that they suggest, which the imperialistic English mind is incapable of fathoming, is also supported by leitmotifs, and Forster again uses leitmotifs in this novel for characterization. Thus Fielding is repeatedly connected with his desire to *travel lightly*, which of course suggests his whole desire to be without a cumbersome past and present in terms of antiquated English ideology. Miss Quested's touristy desire to "see the real India" becomes a leitmotif connected with her and helps the reader to understand her naiveté in terms of her English educational background. In this novel the leitmotifs, when they do appear, are very similar to Forster's earlier uses of them in his pre-World War I novels. His rhythmic aesthetic for the novel, then, which necessitated the Wagnerian uses of leitmotif, reached its height with *Howards End*. But Forster again uses a tripartite structure in *A Passage to India*—Mosque, Caves, Temple. This is a form he had used in *The Longest Journey's* Cambridge, Sawston, and Wiltshire sections, but here it is used to suggest a religious progression. The three social groups present in the novel, Moslem, Hindu, and English, also reflect this three-part form. While the three sections of the novel are joined by a pattern of leitmotifs, they are not so thickly clustered as in earlier works. However, *Howards End* uses motifs in a more complex way to communicate many more aspects of characterization and theme than Forster attempts in *Passage*.

*Passage* is, in many ways, Forster's *Parsifal*, for it involves the search of an innocent (Mrs. Moore) for enlightenment in the

Malabar Caves. Wagner's Parsifal does find enlightenment and peace, but in the novel the search becomes confused and frustrated. Miss Quested, the frustrated spinster, has a bout of sexual hysteria that results in her silly accusation against Dr. Aziz. Mrs. Moore sees a profound reality in the caves, but becomes bitter and withdrawn by the experience. By the end of the novel Dr. Aziz and Cecil Fielding try again at friendship but fail. "'No, not yet,' and the sky said, 'No, not there.'"[17] This is the last sentence of the novel and suggests that Forster's hope for the brotherhood of men lies in the distant future, for there is too much bad blood between them at present. Forster is also suggesting that friendship demands equality and because the British are rulers in India they can have no real friendship with the Indian people. The tragedy of the novel is that so few of them want it. But what is Wagnerian about all this? The search for enlightenment is certainly not peculiar to Wagner's operas. But the form here, the rhythm of motifs joining together the three major sections of the novel, is Wagnerian. The search for the real India, the mystery of the Malabar Caves, the attempt to "travel lightly," and the search for true friendship recur nonrandomly throughout the three major subdivisions of the novel—and with all the rhythmic force of a bass drum.

With *Maurice* (1971) we come to the decline of Forster's art, at least in terms of construction. His ideal for the rhythmic novel is not fulfilled in *Maurice*, for he seems too personally involved in his desire to write about his own homosexuality to maintain enough aesthetic distance from his subject matter. Thomas Mann's Tonio Kröger said that if a writer is too involved in a piece of fiction he will probably produce a sentimental mess. While this is not completely true of *Maurice*, the final result is an interesting novel that is better propaganda than art. The novel's thinness and lack of rhythmic reverberation are a result of its failure to use the structural device that Forster used for all his greatest fiction, the leitmotif. We have seen that while this was certainly not a uniquely Wagnerian device but had occurred in literature and music before the twentieth century, Forster's distinctive and complex use of the technique is highly reminiscent of Wagner's use of it. This, coupled with Forster's statements in the *Paris Review* interview and his own love of music, leads one to see the Wagnerian uses of leitmotif in all of Forster's greatest novels. Why did he not also use it in *Maurice*? Aside from the possibility that he had lost aesthetic distance, perhaps he was just tired of a technique that he had mastered in *Howards End* and *A Passage to India*, and wanted to experiment with something more spontaneous and less artificial. Here Forster abandons the three-part structure he was so fond of and uses four major parts instead—surely another sign of experimentation in addition to the absence of motifs.

Forster's uses of Wagner, then, varied from allusions for purposes of setting, theme, and comedy to rhythmic structuring through extensive and subtle uses of leitmotifs. *Howards End* uses the motif in its most complex literary form, while his other novels are not so purposeful in this regard. Forster's love of Wagnerian opera accounts for the form of his greatest novels.

On December 1, 1951, Benjamin Britten's *Billy Budd* premiered at Covent Garden. After years of using an originally operatic form in his fiction, Forster finally attempted opera itself as one of the two librettists of this work. From what Britten has said, Forster was primarily responsible for the libretto. Predictably, he used verbal leitmotifs for the text of the opera and Britten provided musical equivalents for most of them. "Man of war," "Rights of man," "O heave," "a floating republic," "Baby Billy," "Mutiny," "pretty twinkling," "the mist," "Starry Vere," "this fragment of earth"—all these phrases recur in the opera, and Britten clothes each with a distinctive musical motif to give his opera a form based on two basic chords and the manipulation of about twenty motifs. These literary and musical motifs express the main themes of the opera—the conflicts between good and evil, brute power and the rights of man, youth and old age, and beauty and ugliness. Benjamin Britten and E. M. Forster created a music-drama in the Wagnerian sense rather than a conventional opera.

## Notes

1. E. M. Forster, *Two Cheers for Democracy* (New York, 1938, 1951), p. 128.
2. Malcomm Cowley, ed., *Writers at Work: The Paris Review Interviews* (New York, 1957), p. 31.
3. E. M. Forster, *Aspects of the Novel* (New York, 1927, 1954), p. 168.
4. Wilfred Stone, *The Cave and the Mountain, A Study of E. M. Forster* (Stanford, Calif. 1966), p. 109.
5. Forster, *Two Cheers for Democracy*, p. 130.
6. Benjamin Britten, ''Some Notes on Forster and Music,'' in Oliver Stallybrass, ed., *Aspects of E. M. Forster* (New York, 1969), p. 82.
7. Forster, *Two Cheers for Democracy*, p. 107.
8. Ibid., p. 71.
9. See Stone's *The Cave*; Alan Wilde's *Art and Order: A Study of E. M. Forster* (New York, 1964); and J. B. Beer's *The Achievement of E. M. Forster* (London, 1962).
10. E. M. Forster, *The Collective Tales of E. M. Forster* (New York, 1959), pp. 27-28. Hereafter referred to in the text.
11. E. M. Forster, *Where Angels Fear to Tread* (New York, 1920), p. 5. Hereafter referred to in the text.
12. E. M. Forster, *The Longest Journey* (New York, 1962), p. 4. Hereafter referred to in the text.
13. E. M. Forster, *A Room with a View* (New York, n.d.), p. 150. Hereafter referred to in the text.
14. Stone, *The Cave*, p. 226.
15. E. M. Forster, *Howards End* (New York, 1921), pp. 39-40. Hereafter referred to in the text.
16. Stone, *The Cave*, p. 268.
17. E. M. Forster, *A Passage to India* (New York, 1952), p. 322. Hereafter referred to in the text.

4

# Mythic Characterization: Richard Wagner and Virginia Woolf

Richard Wagner's operas had a pronounced influence upon some of the novels of Virginia Woolf. *The Voyage Out* (1915), *Jacob's Room* (1922), *The Waves* (1931), and *The Years* (1937) all owe something to Wagnerian opera. These works span most of Woolf's writing career, which implies a prolonged and probably changing influence, but the time gaps between the works also allow for some differences in her uses of the operas. She had a lasting fascination with the person of heroic potential, the influence of such a person upon the ordinary man, the suddenness of death, and the pervasive presence of the dead among the living. All these themes are archetypal rather than social or economic, and they lend themselves to mythic treatment. And her curiosity about the artistic uses of myth naturally drew her to Wagner's mythic operas. Since Woolf often went to concerts and operas when she was in London, her lifelong involvement with music would also attract her to the composer, especially given the exalted opinion of his works and the frequency of their performance in London during her most formative years. The combination of myth and music, embodied so consummately in his operas, links two of her special interests. Given these interests, his achievements before her, and the times, the two artists were fated for a union of some sort.

But how did Virginia Woolf get to know about these operas in the first place? The earliest source for her knowledge probably came from her immediate family. Her father, Sir Leslie Stephen, as an enlightened Victorian, certainly knew Wagnerian opera, as did many of his intellectual friends.[1] Wagner was considered very avant-garde in the last third of the nineteenth century and his summer festival at Bayreuth was a Mecca for those who considered themselves knowledgeable about new directions in the arts. Leonard Woolf mentions in his autobiography that when he first met the Stephen family both brothers and sisters were very fond of Wagner, had been to Bayreuth, and had seen many Wagnerian productions at Covent Garden. Leonard Woolf also adds that he himself was not very fond of these operas and did not particularly relish seeing them, but Virginia and her sister enjoyed them immensely and went often. As he reports in *Beginning Again*: "Virginia and Adrian with Saxon Sidney-Turner used to go, almost ritualistically, to the great Wagner festival at Bayreuth."[2] Leonard Woolf gives his own opinion of the composer on the next page: "There are, as I said, moments of beauty and excitement in the *Ring*; there is still more, perhaps, to be said for the early Wagner, as in *Lohengrin*, and for the *Meistersinger*. But I did not enjoy the *Ring* in my box, with Virginia by my side, in 1911, and *Tristan* and *Parsifal* when I came to hear them repelled me and far outdid the *Ring* with tediousness and monotony."[3] Leonard was obviously not very fond of Wagnerian opera, but his attitude was not typical in 1911, although it was in 1939.

Despite Leonard's opinions to the contrary, Virginia Woolf was acting in entire accord with the intellectual and artistic interests of her age. During the Edwardian period particularly, anyone who considered himself at all intellectual had to know something about Wagner; this was notably true of artistically elite circles like the

Bloomsbury Group. So, as a young thinking person and as the daughter of her father, Virginia Woolf was a product of her environment in this regard. Her own Wagnerism is reflected in much of her correspondence with Lytton Strachey, to whom she writes in 1908: "I have got so miserably involved in opera and the German language."[4] Several times throughout these years she writes Strachey that she has been going to the opera, usually Wagner. Though generally favorable, her remarks are sometimes critical as well. On February 9, 1909, she writes rather sardonically: "We are just half dazed from the opera—six solid hours of it—and if were properly edited one might get through in 30 minutes."[5] Given the length of time, there could have been but one composer intended by that comment.

Also in 1909 Virginia Woolf wrote a long article for the London *Times*, entitled "Impressions at Bayreuth," that describes the Bayreuth festival's season of 1909 for Londoners who were unable to get there. In the process of reporting her reactions to the performances, she demonstrates a profound knowledge of Wagnerian opera and Wagnerian production; this article was written by someone who knew the operas well. At the end of the essay she summarized: "Thus, in the final impression of Bayreuth this year, beauty is still triumphant, although the actual performances (if we except *Götterdämmerung*, which remains to be heard) have been below the level of many that have been given in London. Details which have contributed to this disappointment—that the orchestra was weak, that there were few great singers, and that the prompter whispered incessantly—might be furnished; but to refrain seems better, since they must cross the channel."[6] Aside from the evaluations, the article spends most of its time with *Parsifal*, which Woolf especially liked. Here is her personal reaction to the 1909 Bayreuth production of the opera: "Somehow Wagner has conveyed the desire of the Knights for the Grail in such a way that the intense emotion of human beings is combined with the unearthly nature of the thing they seek. It tears us, as we hear it, as though its wings were sharply edged. Again, feelings of the kind that are equally diffused and felt for one object in common create an impression of largeness and, when the music is played as it was played on the night of the 11th, of an overwhelming unity. The grail seems to burn through all superincumbences; the music is intimate in a sense that none other is; one is fired with emotion and yet possessed with tranquility at the same time, for the words are continued by the music so that we hardly notice the transition. It may be that those exalted emotions, which belong to the essence of our being, and are rarely expressed, are those that are best translated by music."[7] While her discussion of the opera's basic dichotomy of emotional appeal is highly perceptive, the desire to verbalize its effect implies an essentially literary response. Her final comment about music and literature sustains this impression of her as a music-lover with literary interests. Although she was fond of the other operas as well, "Impressions at Bayreuth" indicates that *Parsifal* had a special hold on her emotions, a hold that we shall see reflected in her fiction.

Virginia Woolf's trip to Bayreuth in August 1909 is also described and analyzed by Quentin Bell in his biography of her. In Volume 1 of his book he says of the trip: "I must explain why Virginia was there in the month of August 1909. In later years it was the last place in which one would have expected to find her. She was not, in any strict sense, musical. She played no instrument; I do not think that she could follow a score with any deep comprehension. Music, it is true, delighted her; she enjoyed the family pianola (when Adrian did not play it for too long), and she was later to enjoy the gramophone; it formed a background to her musings, a theme for her pen; during the period at which Adrian kept a diary she was frequently at concerts and very frequently at the opera, which she enjoyed as a spectacle and a social event. But her taste for opera was, as Adrian's had been, probably stimulated by Saxon; certainly he must have been responsible for the marked homage which she now paid to Wagner, for Saxon was, and always remained, a fervent Wagnerian."[8] Quentin Bell underestimates her musical interest; she went to far too many operas and concerts to regard them simply as background music or social events. There are so many allusions to music in her fiction that, although she was not a professional musician, the art was clearly important to her.

In the second volume of his biography Bell also describes one of the last times Virginia saw the complete *Ring*, with decidedly disastrous results. It was in 1913 and weeks before one of her bouts with insanity, hardly the right time for the complexities of the whole tetralogy. Bell reports: "They [Virginia and Leonard] remained prudently at Asham for the greater part of April and May, but went back to London to attend the *Ring* at Covent Garden, which Virginia then vowed she would never do again: 'my eyes are bruised, my ears dulled, my brain a mere pudding of pulp—O the noise, the heat, & the brawling sentimentality, which used once to carry me away, & now leaves me sitting perfectly still.' "[9] Quentin Bell suggests that this was her final view of Wagnerian opera; but the repeated references to it in her later work, especially in *The Years*, imply that her negative reaction in 1913 was primarily a result of her precarious psychological state at the time. But it must be noted that by the 20s her Wagnerism had certainly cooled, as it had among English intellectuals generally.

Aside from the biographical facts about Virginia Woolf's awareness of Wagner, the most important source for such information is really her novels. The variety and sheer quantity of their Wagnerian allusions prove conclusively that she knew the operas well. The only source on this subject is William Blissett, specifically in his article "Wagnerian Fiction in English," which appeared in *Criticism* in 1963. Blissett's useful essay mentions that Virginia Woolf was influenced by Wagner and points out where many of the allusions occur in her fiction,[10] but after pointing them out he does not explore their specific functions in the novels. Hence I would like to start where Blissett left off, by investigating why the allusions are there and what artistic purpose they serve.

Wagnerian references exist significantly in four of her novels: *The Voyage Out, Jacob's Room, The Waves*, and *The Years*. Let us now look at each of them.

There are many direct references to Wagner in Woolf's first novel, *The Voyage Out*, but why are they there? First of all, she uses many of them to establish the intellectual climate of the society and class she is trying to portray. Although the novel was first published in 1915, it depicts late Victorian or early Edwardian society, which was notably Wagnerian in its operatic tastes. Another noticeable aspect of the allusions is that they first cluster around Rachel and Mrs. Dalloway. The following long passage, which appears early in the novel, exemplifies this:

> "You play?" said Mrs. Dalloway to Mrs. Ambrose, taking up the score of *Tristan* which lay on the table.
>
> "My niece does," said Helen, laying her hand on Rachel's shoulder.
>
> "Oh, how I envy you!" Clarissa addressed Rachel for the first time. "D'you remember this? Isn't it divine?" She played a bar or two with ringed fingers upon the page.
>
> "And then Tristan goes like this, and Isolde! Have you been to Bayreuth?"
>
> "No, I haven't," said Rachel.
>
> "Then, that's still to come. I shall never forget my first *Parsifal*—a grilling August day, and those fat old German women, come in their stuffy high frocks, and then the dark theatre, and the music beginning, and one couldn't help sobbing. A kind man went and fetched me water, I remember; and I could only cry on his shoulder! It caught me here" (she touched her throat). "It's like nothing else in the world! But where's your piano?"
>
> "It's in another room," Rachel explained.
>
> "But you will play to us?" Clarissa entreated. "I can't imagine anything nicer than to sit out in the moonlight and listen to music—only sounds too like a schoolgirl! You know," she said, turning to Helen a little mysteriously, "I don't think music's altogether good for people—I'm afraid not."
>
> "Too great a strain?" asked Helen.

> "Too emotional," said Clarissa. "One notices it at once when a boy or girl takes up music as a profession. Sir William Broadley told me just the same thing. Don't you hate the kind of attitudes people go into over Wagner—like this—" She cast her eyes to the ceiling, clasped her hands, and assumed a look of intensity. "It really doesn't mean that they appreciate him; in fact, I always think it's the other way round. The people who really care about an art are always the least affected."[11]

This conversation reflects some of the musical interests of the upper-middle classes during the turn of the century, but notice how the allusions help to characterize Mrs. Dalloway as well. Her reaction to her first *Parsifal* at Bayreuth sounds laughably like that of the people she herself criticizes at the end of the passage, while her agreement with Sir Broadley on the detrimental aspects of music for the young adds to the fatuous effect. But on the other hand Mrs. Dalloway does have a sincerely responsive appreciation of the operas, so this is a two-edged sword that Woolf is wielding. Her "Impressions at Beyreuth" essay of 1909 includes reactions to *Parsifal* that are similar to Mrs. Dalloway's, though not so extreme.

When Rachel Vinrace falls in love with Terence Hewet, the central relationship in the novel, a pattern of allusions to *Tristan und Isolde* becomes prominent. The characters themselves do not fit neatly into this framework; Rachel lacks the impetuous fatalism of Isolde and Terence's position as Cambridge student is very different from that of the world-weary Tristan. But like the Wagnerian lovers, this couple is motivated consistently by passion and nothing else, and Woolf solidifies this connection with references to *Tristan und Isolde*. In the second chapter Rachel is reading a translation of Wagner's libretto for *Tristan* and later we discover, along with Mrs. Dalloway, the score of the opera lying on Rachel's piano. She is fond of Wagner and often plays *Tristan* while she is on the ship. Water is often in the novel's setting, and in fact much of the action occurs on board ship. The first act of *Tristan und Isolde* also takes place on board ship, where the lovers become aware of their mutual passion. The connection is strengthened by the treatment of Rachel's death and her lover's response to it. The following passage relates Terence's thoughts while she dies: "The longer he sat there the more profoundly was he conscious of the peace invading every corner of his soul. Once he held his breath and listened acutely . . . She had ceased to breathe. So much the better—this was death. It was nothing; it was to cease to breathe. It was happiness, it was perfect happiness. They had now what they had always wanted to have, the union which had been impossible while they lived" (p. 353). It is this strange combination of love and death that gives the passage its essential similarity to Wagner's *Tristan*. Terence feels, as Tristan did during the *Liebesnacht*, that their love can be totally fulfilled only in death. The last sentence in this passage parallels exactly Tristan's statement during the *Liebesnacht*:

> Was stürbe dem Tod, als was uns stört,
> was Tristan wehrt, Isolde immer zu lieben,
> ewig ihr nur zu leben?
>
> What could death destroy but what impedes us,
> that hinders Tristan from loving Isolde
> forever, and living but for her.

The totality and finality of such a passion also motivates Rachel and Terence, for their love is never conceived out of economics, social status, or companionship, but passion alone. The novel's ending could easily have lapsed into contrived melodrama, but Woolf's use of Wagnerian references give the love a philosophical import as well as a mythic dimension. Terence and Rachel's situation, by being compared to Tristan and Isolde's, is thereby elevated. By the end of the novel Terence has ceased to be the bookish Cambridge undergraduate and has experienced a death-fulfilled, passionate love. The Wagnerian materials in *The Voyage Out* have helped Woolf to present her characters, expand them, and comment upon the import of their situations.

*Jacob's Room*, also set in the late Victorian period, again uses Wagner as part of the artistic background. This passage also indicates the historical setting: "The autumn season was in full swing. Tristan was twitching his rug up under his armpits twice a week; Isolde waved her scarf in miraculous sympathy with the conductor's baton. In all parts of the house were to be found pink faces and glittering breasts. When a Royal hand attached to an invisible body slipped out and withdrew the red and white bouquet reposing on the scarlet ledge, the Queen of England seemed a name worth dying for."[12] The satirical note in this passage is a product of Woolf's satirical attitude toward many of the Victorian period's tastes and formalities, like going to the "Opera," the ceremony of Queen Victoria's entrance, and her traditional bouquet of red and white carnations. The tone reflects the Bloomsbury attitude toward Victorianism, especially Lytton Strachey's. Virginia Woolf was very fond of *Eminent Victorians* and shared many of its author's views. Yet satire is not the only intent of this passage because it also dramatizes Wagner's high place in the artistic tastes of the novel's social class and time.

In her famous essay "Mr. Bennett and Mrs. Brown," as well as in her novels, Woolf indicates a deep concern for the problems of characterization. She solves them rather uniquely in *Jacob's Room* and Wagner helps her here too: " 'Distinction'—Mrs. Durrant said that Jacob Flanders was 'distinguished-looking.' 'Extremely awkward,' she said, 'but so distinguished-looking.' Seeing him for the first time that no doubt is the word for him. Lying back in his chair, taking his pipe from his lips, and saying to Bonamy: 'About this opera now' (for they had done with indecency). 'This fellow Wagner' . . . distinction was one of the words to use naturally" (p. 70). The budding late-Victorian intellectual, fresh from Cambridge—this is how Jacob is being portrayed and his interest in new music reflects this. His curiosity about "this fellow Wagner" is entirely in keeping with the interests of intellectuals in the age Woolf is describing. The whole concept of *distinction* is another aspect of the upper social classes of the period and the passage indicates a rather rigid class structure. Woolf's problems with characterization are especially complex in this novel because she is writing around an apparently empty space; here the concept of *room* is central, for we see Jacob's surroundings, his figurative room, without ever entering his mind directly. But this approach has special advantages, for Jacob himself becomes more distanced and mythic because of the barriers that Woolf has created between us and him. She will use this same approach later for Percival in *The Waves*; but there she achieves greater subtlety, in part because she uses Wagner much more in that novel.

Wagner's influence on *The Waves* (1931) is pervasive, despite the fact that his name never appears, unlike the previous books I have discussed. The effect begins with the italicized descriptions of the progression of the sun and the movements of the sea that open each of the chapters. The novel begins: "The sun had not yet risen. The sea was indistinguishable from the sky."[13] The main function of these lighting references is structural; the progression of the sun from predawn darkness to noon and then sunset and predawn darkness again gives the novel a form. The progression of time is suggested, as well as its corollary, death. But the effect is circular and the last chapter begins: "Now the sun had sunk. Sky and sea were indistinguishable. The waves breaking spread their white fans far out over the shore, sent white shadows into the recesses of sonorous caves and then rolled back sighing over the shingle" (p. 340). The indistinguishability of sea and sky begins and ends the novel. The cyclical movement of the waves, which "rolled back sighing," reinforces the circular movement of the lighting. The sound and rhythm of the sea appear repeatedly in the novel because this rhythm is central to its meaning, as the title suggests. The symbolic combination of water with predawn darkness suggests both death and rebirth, which is very similar to Wagner's use of light and water in *Der Ring des Nibelungen*. That vast tetralogy also begins and ends in the darkness before the dawn, and rippling water (supported by rhythmic water music) is on stage for both scenes as well. *Das Rheingold* opens at the

says: "It is Percival I need; for it is Percival who inspires poetry" (pp. 201-2). To inspire poetry is a traditional role of the epic hero. Later in the novel Neville says of him: "Now is our festival; now we are together. But without Percival there is no solidity. We are silhouettes, hollow phantoms moving mistily without a background" (p. 259). When Percival is about to leave for India, Bernard says: "We have come together, at a particular time, to this particular spot. We are drawn into this communion by some deep, some common emotion. Shall we call it, conveniently, 'love'? Shall we say 'love of Percival' because Percival is going to India?" (pp. 262-63). Percival, these passages imply, is a cohesive force for the six characters because he brings them together and gives their lives happiness and meaning. Bernard summarizes his effect later in the novel: "He is a hero. Oh, yes, that is not to be denied, and when he takes his seat by Susan, whom he loves, the occasion is crowned. We who yelp like jackals biting at each other's heels now assume the sober and confident air of soldiers in the presence of their captain" (p. 260). Once again Percival is described as heroic, and a stabilizing and ordering force for the group. Later in the novel, while he is in India, Bernard envisions him there: "But now, behold, Percival advances. . . . By applying the standards of the West, by using the violent language that is natural to him, the bullock-cart is righted in less than five minutes. The Oriental problem is solved. He rides on; the multitude cluster round him, regarding him as if he were—what indeed he is—a God" (p. 269). This passage says a great deal about how Bernard sees Percival. He is being described, as he was before, in heroic terms, for the horse and the standard he represents are typical symbols of the hero. Bernard even imagines Percival deified and worshiped by the natives.

But ultimately Percival is a victimized rather than conquering hero. Harvena Richter says of him: "His young manhood is to be sacrificed, for he will die in India . . . through the ritual enactment of the myth of the sacrifice of the beloved."[15] Percival's death is indeed mythic, an impression reinforced by the poetic language used to describe his end: "'He is dead,' said Neville. 'He fell. His horse tripped. He was thrown. The sails of the world have swung round and caught me on the head. All is over. The lights of the world have gone out . . . . His horse stumbled; he was thrown. The flashing trees and white rails went up in a shower. There was a surge; a drumming in his ears. Then the blow; the world crashed; he breathed heavily. He died where he fell'" (p. 280). Percival experiences death passively: "he was thrown . . . he was thrown," Neville repeats. He imagines all of nature in upheaval and grieving over the death of his hero. The pathetic fallacy and epic hyperboles are used to exalt Percival and the significance of his undeserved, sacrificial death. Wagner's Parsifal, although he is not dead by the end of the opera, is also a sacrificial figure. Amfortas's symbolic wound, a result of his sin of lust, has weakened the whole Grail brotherhood. Wagner's Parsifal, "*der reine Tor*," is a born fool who must learn pity through suffering if he is to save the Grail brotherhood. While he does this by the third act of the opera, Woolf's Percival is destroyed. However, both characters suffer and sacrifice. Thus Percival's death profoundly affects all the other characters in the novel, because they have all lost something as a result of his death but something has been gained as well. Percival's death has a dual meaning, which adds to the character's mythic position in the novel.

Bernard says: "My son is born; Percival is dead" (p. 281). Death, then, is connected with new life. Later in the novel Louis also suggests this connection: "Percival was flowering with green leaves and was laid in the earth with all his branches still sighing in the summer wind" (p. 317). Louis does not imagine Percival as a corpse but resurrected; his very burial is surrounded with images of greenery and renewed life. This aspect of him is reinforced by the many references to crosses and crucifixes in the novel. The following passage spoken by Bernard is a highly concentrated example of what recurs throughout *The Waves*: "So Neville, at school, in the dim chapel, raged at the sight of the rector's crucifix. I, who am always distracted, . . . at once make up a story and so obliterate the angles of the crucifix'' (p. 305). Usually crosses are connected with figures of authority, as in this passage, but they suggest the Christian myth of sacrificial death and resurrection as well. The French critic Maxime Chastaing has attempted to prove that Percival is a Christ figure,[16] and all the references to crosses in the novel help to support his premise. Another possible referent is Wagner's Parsifal, for he also embodies sacrificial and resurrecting characteristics. Parsifal endangers himself and thereby saves the Grail brotherhood, and by the end of the opera he can offer the brotherhood the life-giving properties of the Grail. Percival has also been sacrificed and resurrected: generally, in terms of all the cyclical images in the novel like light and the rings, and specifically, because of his continued influence on the six characters after his death.

But how can we be sure that it is Wagner's Parsifal that is being referred to in the novel and not Malory's or even Jessie Weston's in *From Ritual to Romance*? First, both Malory's and Weston's works include many other figures, with Parsifal as a subsidiary concern, but he is central to Wagner's version. Moreover, these other works do not portray Parsifal as a sacrificial victim, as Wagner does. But the most convincing reason is a musical allusion to the opera that appears, significantly, in the last chapter of the novel. Early in Bernard's final monologue, he says: ''Here again there should be music. Not that wild hunting song, Percival's music; but a painful, guttural, visceral, also soaring, lark-like, pealing song'' (p. 350). The ''hunting song'' for Percival is an allusion to Wagner's Parsifal, for hunting music is used when he first appears in Act I after having killed one of the sacred swans. Woolf's allusion to this music, in addition to the other similarities noticed, provides strong evidence that Wagner's Parsifal is the character she is referring to in *The Waves* and connecting with her Percival.

What, finally, have these Wagnerian patterns done for this novel? The references to the *Ring* provide a parallel with the circular structure, water imagery, lighting descriptions, and ring symbolism in the novel and thereby give it a mythic dimension that it would otherwise lack. Through these parallels to the *Ring*, Woolf is able to add greater scope and meaning to her novel. As a result, the simple progression of a day becomes more epic and has a wider range of references, the lighting in the novel acquires structural significance, and water rhythms and ring images take on greater force. Woolf's borrowings from Wagner's *Ring* make her novel reverberate with epic implications that it would otherwise lack. *Parsifal*, on the other hand, helps her to portray the complex nature of her hero. Here her task is especially difficult because we never enter Percival's mind directly nor hear him speak. Given his lack of immediacy, the many parallels with Wagner's Parsifal help Woolf to dramatize the dual characteristics of sacrifice and resurrection in her own Percival. The heroic and mythic dimensions of her hero become both explained and enhanced by his similarity to Wagner's Parsifal.

*The Years* (1937) is the last of Woolf's works to show a significant Wagnerian influence. Unlike *The Waves*, this novel mentions Wagner specifically in the text and in this way resembles *The Voyage Out* and *Jacob's Room*. Also unlike the more complex *The Waves, The Years* is a historical and generational novel. In the passage below, Woolf characterizes the period of her chapter (1910) as well as the social position of her characters at that time: "'I'm so sorry,' she [Kitty] apologised, 'to be so late. And for coming in these ridiculous clothes,' she added, touching her cloak. She did look strange, dressed in evening dress in the broad daylight. There was something shining in her hair. 'The Opera?' said Martin as she sat down beside him. 'Yes,' she said briefly."[17] Kitty is behaving like an enlightened Edwardian lady of the upper classes by going to the Opera (with a capital *O*), and going properly bejeweled and begowned. It is not insignificant that the opera in this case is Wagner's *Siegfried*. The Edwardian society that Woolf has been portraying and the mythic world of *Siegfried* are contrasted several pages later when we read of Kitty's reaction to the opera: "Here the curtain went up. She leant forward and looked at the stage. The dwarf was hammering at the sword. Hammer, hammer, hammer, he went with little short, sharp strokes.... But here was Siegfried. She leant forward. Dressed in leopardskins, very fat, with nut-brown thighs, leading a bear—here he was. She liked the fat bouncing young man in his flaxen wig; his voice was magnificent. Hammer, hammer, hammer he went. She leant back again. What did that make her think of. A young man who came into a room with shavings in his hair... and there was a sound of hammering in the garden. And then a boy came in with shavings in his hair. And she had wanted him to kiss her. Or was it the farm hand up at Carter's, when old Carter had loomed up suddenly leading a bull with a ring through its nose? 'That's the sort of life I like,' she thought, taking up her opera-glasses. 'That's the sort of person I am'" (pp. 183-84). Through contrast this passage indicates some of the formalities and artificialities of the Edwardian period that by 1937 were already dated. The primal emotions and natural settings of *Siegfried* are worlds away from the society Kitty lives in, the upper classes in the London of 1910. This was Woolf's own family background and she knew the limitations of this class well.

This passage tells us much about the character of Kitty as well as her social class at the time. Siegfried's singing reminds her of an incident in her past which also involved hammering. The young man "with shavings in his hair," coupled with the bull, suggests male sexuality. Her unsatisfied desire for his kiss dramatizes her wish for a freer sexuality, freed from the rigid class structure of Edwardian London. "That's the sort of person I am," she asserts at the end of this passage. Her thoughts are generated by watching Siegfried on stage; they place her in a position similar to Brünnhilde's in the first act of this opera, asleep and awaiting the mythic hero to awaken her. By the end of the opera Brünnhilde has been roused to both the light of day and Siegfried's passionate love, but Kitty's fate is more complex. By the end of the novel she is a seventy-year-old widow. "She lived alone now, in the north. '... and I daresay I'm better off as I am,' she added, half to herself, 'with just a boy to chop up wood'" (p. 418). This boy connects handily with the one "with shavings in his hair," as well as with Siegfried. She seems to have attained her desire for a simple rural life, complete with a young man. But such a final fulfillment is surely intended ironically, considering her age. Her end is not so heroic as Brünnhilde's and the Wagnerian connection creates a special irony here.

The passage above contains several references to the hammerings on stage during Act I, scene 1 of *Siegfried*. They become especially pronounced after Kitty's stream-of-consciousness vision and during her description of the forging music, which is the finale of the opera's first act. During this exciting section Siegfried forges his sword, Nothung. Here is the opening of the forging music in the piano-vocal score:

Siegfried's downward-leaping octave is always connected with Nothung. The staccati and trills in the orchestra marvelously suggest the mounting fire used to forge the sword. Kitty describes this forging music, which ends the first act of *Siegfried*, and its effect on her in this passage: "The music excited her. It was magnificent. Siegfried took the broken pieces of the sword and blew on the fire and hammered, hammered, hammered. The singing, the hammering, and the fire leaping all went on at the same time. Quicker and quicker, more and more rhythmically, more and more triumphantly he hammered, until at last up he swung the sword high above his head and brought it down—crack! The anvil burst asunder. And then he brandished the sword over his head and shouted and sang! and the music rushed higher and higher; and the curtain fell" (pp. 184-85). Siegfried's forging music starts a series of references to hammering and fire sparks in the novel. Several pages after this passage Maggie and Sara suddenly hear some loud noise: "Somebody was hammering on the door of the next house. The hammering stopped. Then it began again—hammer, hammer, hammer. They listened" (p. 190). In the "1914" chapter fire sparks recur when Kitty goes to a fireplace: "She dealt the coal a blow, and the sparks went volleying up the chimney. She was irritable; she was restless. Time was passing" (p. 264). In the next chapter, "1917," the same Siegfried-derived motif appears: "Maggie took the poker and struck the wood blocks. The sparks went volleying up the chimney in a shower of gold eyes" (p. 294). Siegfried's forging music has started a series of hammerings and fire sparks. Woolf uses them as a means of structuring her long, generational novel, which spans fifty-seven years.

J. K. Johnstone, in his chapter on Virginia Woolf in *The Bloomsbury Group*, also discusses part of this pattern, although he prefers to call it a rhythm. He says that "hammering—Jo Robson hammering nails in a hencoop, the hammering in *Siegfried*, a drunken man hammering on a door near Sara and Maggie Pargiter's flat—develops into a modest 'rhythm.'"[18] It is through patterns such as these that Virginia Woolf gives *The Years* a form.

She avoids the typically Victorian approach of structuring the novel around its plot and, like a true modern, prefers symbols and images. Wagner's *Siegfried* has provided her with a source of aural and visual images, hammering and fire sparks. In addition to this, Woolf has employed Wagnerian allusions in the novel as a means of characterization, and they help her to portray a society and also the plight of a particular woman within that class. Kitty's stream-of-consciousness vision, generated by the first act of *Siegfried*, tells us much about her difficulties in trying to fit into the urban social fabric of the London of 1910. Wagner's treatment of the Siegfried myth reminds Kitty of her own nonmythic world.

*The Years*, then, uses Wagnerian allusions rather as *The Voyage Out* did, as a means of characterizing an age, a social class within that age, and particular people as well. In both novels the *Ring* defines a mythic and heroic world that contrasts sharply with the social realities portrayed. *Jacob's Room*, on the other hand, uses the allusions mainly as a means of characterizing Jacob and Bonamy as young Cambridge intellectuals who are curious about serious music. *The Waves*, however, employs Wagnerian patterns most profoundly. The *Ring* provides the novel with examples of lighting, imagery, rhythm, and structure. Also, the duality of Percival and Parsifal helps to portray a sacrificial and resurrecting hero in the novel. By the end of *The Waves* Percival's life is over, but his mythic existence continues to influence the other characters. Virginia Woolf, then, not only knew Wagner's operas intimately but used them to help her create whole dimensions of meaning in several of her best novels and to serve as an allusive source for some of her penetrating characterizations. In her famous essay "Mr. Bennett and Mrs. Brown" she had talked about the inadequacy of older methods of capturing the human mind on paper. Wagnerian opera provided her with new sources of materials, especially mythic ones, and, most important, methods for using them in characterization. Like a true modern, Virginia Woolf was determined to portray in literature the human psyche in all its complexity, and this goal led her to many subtle methods. Among them are Wagnerian allusions.

# NOTES

1. Frederic William Maitland, *The Life and Letters of Leslie Stephen* (New York, 1906), p. 492.
2. Leonard Woolf, *Beginning Again: An Autobiography of the Years 1911 to 1918* (New York, 1963), p. 49.
3. Ibid., p. 50.
4. Virginia Woolf and Lytton Strachey, *Letters*, ed. Leonard Woolf and James Strachey (New York, 1956), p. 11.
5. Ibid., p. 35.
6. Virginia Woolf, ''Impressions at Bayreuth,'' ed. John L. Di Gaetani, *Opera News* (August 1976), p. 23.
7. Ibid.
8. Quentin Bell, *Virginia Woolf, A Biography* (New York, 1972), 1: 149.
9. Ibid., 2: 12.
10. William Blissett, ''Wagnerian Fiction in English,'' *Criticism* 5 (Summer 1963): 242-44, 255-58.
11. Virginia Woolf, *The Voyage Out* (New York, 1948), pp. 47-48. Hereafter referred to in the text.
12. Virginia Woolf, *Jacob's Room* (New York, 1959), p. 68. Hereafter referred to in the text.
13. Virginia Woolf, *The Waves* (New York, 1959), p. 179. Hereafter referred to in the text.
14. Blissett, ''Wagnerian Fiction,'' p. 258.
15. Harvena Richter, *Virginia Woolf: The Inward Voyage* (Princeton, N.J., 1970), p. 126.
16. Maxime Chastaing, *La Philosophie de Virginia Woolf* (Paris, 1951), p. 176.
17. Virginia Woolf, *The Years* (New York, 1965), p. 177. Hereafter referred to in the text.
18. J. K. Johnstone, *The Bloomsbury Group: A Study of E. M. Forster, Lytton Strachey, Virginia Woolf, and their Circle* (New York, 1954), p. 369.

5

# Comic Uses of Myth: Richard Wagner and James Joyce

James Joyce was an opera buff for all of his adult life, and he often said that his favorite kind of music was the sound of a fine tenor voice. He himself had an excellent voice and once thought of becoming a professional singer in Dublin; such a career was suggested by many of his close friends and advisers at his university.[1] However, he rejected the idea because it would have kept him in Dublin, for he knew that he did not have the kind of voice that could attract international attention. The literary life meant for him the freedom of a life on the Continent and away from provincial Ireland. While on the Continent, though, he continued to sing with friends and often went to the opera.

For most of his life Joyce's operatic taste was definitely Italianate. He did, however, go through a Wagnerian phase during his University College days in Dublin, when his prime literary interest was Ibsen and the new drama. In a lecture delivered in 1900 to the university's Literary and Historical Society, on "Drama and Life," Joyce said: "Even the least part of Wagner—his music—is beyond Bellini. Spite of the outcry of these lovers of the past, the masons are building for Drama, an ampler and loftier home, where there shall be light for gloom, and wide porches for drawbridge and keep."[2] This is a highly significant passage, for although Joyce was in his early twenties when he wrote it, it summarizes what was to be his lifelong opinion of Wagner. Partially, he is praising him here because Wagner was a useful name to drop in 1900 among arty circles. But there is more than name-dropping intended, for Joyce did admire the composer, especially as a dramatist. Although Joyce often saw Wagner's operas performed, he came in his maturity to prefer Vincenzo Bellini's music to Wagner's; but in terms of drama, Wagner was one of his lifelong interests. Several pages later in the same essay, Joyce writes: "Every race has made its own myths and it is in these that early drama often finds an outlet. The author of Parsifal has recognized this and hence his work is solid as a rock."[3] Joyce's praise of Wagner is in terms of drama and myth rather than music. In 1902 in an essay on James Clarence Mangan, Joyce makes another allusion to Wagner's *Parsifal*: "That was a strange question which the innocent Parsifal asked—'Who is good?'—and it is recalled to mind when one reads certain criticisms and biographies."[4] This comment implies a thorough knowledge of that opera, and in fact Joyce owned and studied many of the complete scores of Wagner's operas.

Joyce's essays as a university student give us his earliest opinions of Wagner and his operas, but we must look to his correspondence for the broader view of his mature evaluation of the composer. The first reference to Wagner that we find in the three volumes of collected letters (ed. Stuart Gilbert, 1957) is the following entry dated 25 January 1903 and addressed to his mother: "Tell Stannie to send me *at once* (so that I may have it by Thursday night) my copy of Wagner's operas."[5] The next reference occurs in a letter to his brother Stanislaus, dated August 1906: "Last night we heard a band in the piazza Colonna play a selection from *Siegfried*. Very fine" (2: 145). A year later Joyce is again writing to his brother about Wagnerian performances in Italy: "I was going to squander a lira on *The Dusk of the Gods* tonight but am afraid that, in my present pendulous mood, I couldn't stand in the gallery for 3 hours" (2: 213). The idea of squandering a single lira on Wagner's longest and perhaps greatest opera is a clever irony of Joyce's, but only the most hurried or severely cut performance of this opera would last only three hours. Three days later, on 14 February 1907, Joyce did hear this opera in Rome, and he wrote to his brother about it: "I went to the *Dusk of the Gods*. Beside me in the gallery was an elderly man who smelt of garlic. He said it was a colossal opera and that it required great voices. He had heard it in Hamburg. He spoke a few words to me in English, such as, very cold, very good and beautiful. Before me was another man who said Wagner's music was splendid but intended only for Germans. It was all intellect: no heart. Every time the horn motive sounded my garlicy friend twisted to me and said confidently: *Adesso viene Sigfrido*. He yawned much during the third act and went away before the last scene. When Brünnhilde brought on the horse, the latter, being unable to sing, evacuated; whereat the funny Italian disyllable flew from end to end of the gallery. There were many spectators who followed the opera with scores and librettos. On the stairs coming away and in the street I heard many people hum correctly and incorrectly the nine notes of the funeral motive. Nothing in the opera moved me. I have heard the funeral march often before. Only when Siegfried dies I responded from the crown of my head to his cry '*O sposa sacra*.' I suppose there are a few men from time to time who really feel an impulse towards Gawd" (2: 214). Apparently as long as Joyce was in Italy he saw Wagner only in Italian translation, usually severely cut, and often in terrible productions. In this letter Joyce himself describes the sometimes ludicrous results. Despite the comic and satiric tone throughout this marvellous description, Joyce does admit that he was moved at least by Siegfried's final monologue.

Only two weeks later, on 1 March 1907, Joyce went to yet another performance of this opera and again wrote to his brother

Stanislaus about it: "I was about two days making up my mind to go and see the *Dusk of the Gods*. I weighed the cold, the distance, the crush, discomfort, etc. Finally I went and tried to interest myself but was considerably bored. The fault, I believe, is more mine than Wagner's but at the same time I cannot help wondering what relation music like this can possibly have to the gentlemen I was with in the gallery" (2: 337-38) Once again, Joyce has definite reservations about Wagnerian operas in production; yet he has gone to three performances of *Götterdämmerung* within two months, which implies a real interest and some enjoyment despite the reservations. It is interesting too that the future author of *Ulysses* is concerned about the effects of mythic drama on the common man, which suggests his own artistic concerns at the time. Joyce's correspondence also indicates that during his Zurich days he participated in a performance of the quintet from *Die Meistersinger von Nürnberg*, his favorite Wagnerian opera.[6] He wrote to his son Giorgio of the concert and also mentioned an aria from the opera that he especially liked (2: 337-38).

Toward the end of his life, Joyce often went to the opera to hear his favorite tenor, John Sullivan, whom he had first heard in the title role of Wagner's *Tannhäuser* in Paris. In fact, Joyce wrote a clever parody of this opera in 1932 in his essay "From a Banned Writer to a Banned Singer." It is clear, then, that although Joyce's musical and operatic tastes were primarily those of an Italian opera lover, Wagner was often in his thoughts and letters. What especially interested Joyce in the operas was Wagner's use of myth and his attempts to revive the art of the drama as well as music, an interest that is apparent from his first comments on the composer. But except for *Meistersinger*, he rarely warmed to Wagner's music.

We get another insight into Joyce's attitude toward Wagner in the following incident, reported in Ellman's biography: "[Arthur] Symons was to play as central a part in the publication of Joyce's early work as Ezra Pound was to play later. . . . All the arts attracted him [Symons]; in music he was a Wagnerian, and he played for Joyce the Good Friday music from *Parsifal*, remarking in a manner that seemed to Joyce ninetyish, 'When I play Wagner, I am in another world.' "[7] Symons's attitude toward the composer makes a convenient and telling contrast with Joyce's. While the 90s loved the sensual and sensuous quality of Wagner's operas, Joyce appreciated their mythic and dramatic aspects; in fact, he disliked that sensory atmosphere which the symbolists and aesthetes relished. Ellman later reports: "Joyce had no patience with the current adulation of Wagner, objecting that '*Wagner puzza di sesso*' [Wagner stinks of sex]; Bellini, he said, was far better."[8] Still, Joyce went to Wagnerian performances in Rome, Paris, and Zurich—and, as we shall see, his later works contain more and more Wagnerian allusions. But he used the composer as a modern novelist would, not a poet of the 90s.

That Joyce used leitmotifs in his fiction is a cliché of Joycean criticism. A. Walton Litz's *The Art of James Joyce: Method and Design in Ulysses and Finnegans Wake* and Clive Hart's *Structure and Motif in Finnegans Wake* both mention Wagner's leitmotifs in connection with Joyce's methods of structuring his fiction. By the time he was writing they had become a common literary device—assuming that Wagner originated them in the first place, which is highly doubtful. That the French Symbolists as well as Edouard Dujardin were devotees of the Wagnerian leitmotif technique is also well known. Dujardin, who was founder and editor of *La Revue Wagnerienne* and a friend of Joyce's, has said that he consciously modeled his interior monologues on Wagnerian motifs.[9] Although Joyce was never that much of a Wagnerian, he did use leitmotifs more as his works grew increasingly complex, but this is not necessarily Wagnerian. It is impossible to prove that his use of leitmotifs, unlike Forster's, is in any way Wagnerian.

In addition to the use of leitmotifs, Joyce and Wagner had many biographical similarities. William Blissett points them out in the following passage: "Their early struggles in a hinterland of European culture, their marriages (Nora was a happier, more durable

Minna), their exile, the demands they made on the time and purse of their friends, their egotism and empirebuilding, the grandiosity of their artistic ambitions, the time it took them to complete their projects and the completeness of that fulfillment, and, not the least striking of resemblances, the international and polyglot intellectuals that were drawn to them to make a cult of personality as well as the art—all these bring the two into a single, very uncommon, category: the culture-hero as total artist, totally fulfilled."[10] But Joyce's essentially comic art is worlds away from Wagnerian tragedy, and Wagnerian aesthetics is, except for its emphasis on myth, very unlike Joyce's theories of art. Given some of their biographical similarities, Joyce's interest in music and myth, and the reputation of Wagner during the Edwardian period, the attraction that Joyce felt for the composer was very natural. Joycean satire and parody, however, extend even to Wagnerian dramatics, for they help him to achieve a uniquely mythic dimension in his own art.

During the years that Joyce was first hearing the operas of Wagner in Italy, he was also writing *Dubliners*; the first product of his interest in Wagner appears in that work. "A Painful Case," finished in 1905, employs a pattern of references to *Tristan und Isolde*. While it is impossible to establish that Joyce used only Wagner's version of the myth, the times and his current interest in the composer suggest that Wagner is the most probable source. Mr. Duffy, the story's stuffy, middle-aged Tristan, lives in Chapelizod. This town is, according to legend, the home of Isolde, and the word itself is an Anglicization of the French *Chapel d'Iseult*. The pathetic death of Mrs. Sinico is life-giving, for it forces Mr. Duffy finally to realize his responsibility in causing it. She had offered him love, albeit adulterous love, as in the Tristan myth; but Mr. Duffy, a respectable Dubliner, is horrified when she takes his hand and he refuses to have anything more to do with her. The setting in Chapelizod and the situation of adulterous love parallel the Tristan myth. Wagner's lovers are heroic creatures who surrender themselves completely to their passion and are finally destroyed by it. Joyce's Tristan is a bourgeois, Dublin recluse who rejects his Isolde and drives her to alcoholism. The Wagnerian pattern in the story provides an ironic contrast to its characters and situation, but the final effect is a Joycean combination of ridicule and pathos.

In *A Portrait of the Artist as a Young Man* only one passage alludes directly to Wagner, but it is important. "Yes, now, Stephen said. We can't speak here. Come away. They crossed the quadrangle together without speaking. The birdcall from *Siegfried* whistled softly followed them from the steps of the porch. Cranly turned; and Dixon, who had whistled, called out:—Where are you fellows off to? What about that game, Cranly? They parleyed in shouts across the still air about a game of billiards to be played in the Adelphi hotel. Stephen walked on alone and out into the quiet of Kildare Street."[11] In Wagner's *Siegfried* the forest bird does indeed have its own motif:

The forest bird itself is never actually seen by the audience; the part calls for a boy soprano but is usually taken by a female soprano and is sung off-stage, normally from a ladder in the wings so that the audience experiences the illusion of a lovely bird sound coming from high in the branches of a tree. During the forest-murmurs section of Act II, Siegfried hears various bird sounds (created by the orchestra), is intrigued by them, and even tries to imitate them on a reed, with comically inept results. But once he has killed Fafner, the taste of the dragon's blood enables him to understand the sound of the animals. At this point in the opera he can understand bird calls, and at this point the motif of the forest bird switches from the woodwinds in the orchestra to a soprano singing it from the wings. The motif is for the voice in the last half of the second act only; when it appears in the rest of the opera it is produced by the orchestra. The bird's first function is to warn Siegfried not to trust Mime, since Mime is going to try to kill him to get the ring and Fafner's hoard for himself. After Siegfried has killed the evil and bloody-minded dwarf, the forest bird tells him of a beautiful woman sleeping on a rock surrounded with fire, who is the mate Siegfried has been yearning for. The bird tells him the woman will love him if he can only reach her and awaken her. Act II ends with the hero eagerly following the forest bird, which promises to lead him to the sleeping Brünnhilde.

Given this Wagnerian background, we can see that some of it fits into Joyce's *Portrait*. The first function of the bird, to warn Siegfried of Mime's murderous intentions, is what Dixon is doing in the passage quoted earlier. His whistled forest bird motif serves to warn Stephen of Cranly's intentions, which are to try to murder him spiritually by keeping him in Ireland as a faithful follower of the Roman Catholic Church. When Dixon first appears in the novel, he is described briefly: "He had a quiet toneless voice and urbane manners and on a finger of his plump clean hand he displayed at moments a signet ring." (p. 227). His urbanity and careful dress suggest a dandyish type who would probably know the then very fashionable Wagnerian operas. Dixon appears briefly in the last chapter and is portrayed as one of Stephen's witty university friends. When one of the students farts, Dixon asks quietly: "Did an angel speak?" (p. 230). On the next page, when Temple admits to being a bullock, Dixon responds: "And it does you every credit, Temple" (p. 231). Later in the novel Dixon briefly defends the idea of limbo and the Church's doctrine of baptism, but rather lightly. There is nothing in his character that motivates an effort to warn Stephen of Cranly; more consistent with his portrayal is a simple desire to make a sophisticated joke by whistling an opera tune, though Joyce does not indicate whether Stephen Dedalus understood it. But while Dixon's intentions are merely comic, the motif he whistles does work within the novel's larger pattern of entrapment and flight. Despite Cranly's efforts to keep Stephen in Ireland and within the Catholic fold, Stephen avoids these deadly traps and seeks life—like Siegfried's search for Brünnhilde at the end of Act II of the opera. The forest-bird motif helps both of them escape dangerous ambushes. Finally, Stephen has heeded Dixon's clever warning.

Stephen's ashplant cane creates another body of Wagnerian references. The cane first appears in the fourth chapter but becomes most important in the last. In the middle of the final chapter Stephen stands outside his university and contemplates: "The colonnade above him made him think vaguely of an ancient temple and the ashplant on which he leaned wearily of the curved stick of an augur" (p. 225). The ashwood of the cane hints at a Wagnerian connection. In the *Ring* Wotan always carries a spear made of ash, the symbol of his authority, for upon it are carved the rules by which he governs. The fact that Stephen also carries an ash staff suggests, in Wagnerian terms, his desire to wield a Wotan-like authority. While he, of course, does not possess such authority in the novel, the reference is consistent with his pride as an artist, especially in the last chapter. The fact that he has produced nothing except a mediocre villanelle gives an ironic turn to the allusion to Wotan's spear. In *Ulysses*, the ashplant becomes much more important and its functions are more complex and significant.

Another Wagnerian pattern in the novel involves the combination of woman and sea, which becomes prominent at the end of the fourth chapter. There Stephen sees the girl in the water and has a vision of the fertile life of art, as opposed to the death imagery that surrounds his prior meeting with the director of his college, who suggests that he become a Jesuit. At the opening of the meeting, the director is making nooselike coils with the cord of a window blind (pp. 153-54) and his head is described as a "skull" (p. 154). The world of art is connected in Stephen's mind with the girl in the water, while religion is surrounded by death. The combination of woman with water is a Wagnerian pattern, although certainly not only Wagnerian. In *Der Fliegende Holländer* Senta is much attracted to the nautical Dutchman and flees the hunter, Erik. In the last act of *Tristan und Isolde* the wounded Tristan looks out to sea for Isolde and her healing powers. The *Ring* begins and ends with the Rhinemaidens swimming in the Rhine. The combination of the female with water, and its suggestions of fertility, appears often in Wagner's operas. Such a combination also occurs in Joyce's fiction. Molly Bloom's final monologue often mentions water, and Anna Livia Plurabelle becomes the river Liffey at the end of *Finnegans Wake*. Both artists shared a redemptive view of women and both used water to suggest female fertility. One of Joyce's earliest uses of this symbolic combination is Stephen's vision at the end of the fourth chapter of *Portrait*. Though it is impossible to prove conclusively that Wagner was Joyce's only source, the times and his knowledge of the composer suggest Wagnerian opera as a probable source.

Several of the Wagnerian patterns and allusions noticed in *Portrait* also occur in *Ulysses*. In the first chapter Stephen Dedalus's ashplant cane again appears, and it will reappear in many succeeding chapters and become one of the dominant symbols of the novel. Let us first of all look at the fact that Stephen is carrying a cane. Considering the economic situation he finds himself in, is it not a trifle pretentious of him to be sporting a cane? Of course the novel is set in another era, when fashions were different and men did carry canes. But which kinds of men? If a cane was not to help an old or sick person walk, it was purely decorative and considered a bit dandyish, even by people living during the period of the novel. In fact, Stephen is the only person in *Ulysses* who carries a stick, except for the blind man. Stephen is, of course, afraid of dogs and this may be part of the reason for the cane. Also, Joyce himself carried a cane and this may be a personal reference. But he does solidify Stephen's connection with the blind man in the Proteus section when Stephen closes his eyes and uses the cane to feel his way along the beach. Although he uses it as a staff, he does call it in this scene "my ash sword."[12] The cane-carrying itself is consistent with Stephen's characterization as presented at the end of *Portrait* and in *Ulysses*, that of a pretentious young man who wants to be an artist but so far has produced next to nothing and is a fake.

The connection with Wotan's spear operates in this novel, as it did in *Portrait*. Here too Stephen calls it his "augur's rod." In the *Ring* the spear is also connected with lightning and thunder, which are sometimes used for Wotan's entrances. When he calls for Loge to put a magic fire around Brünnhilde at the end of *Die Walküre*, he strikes a rock with his spear to cause lightning. When Stephen uses his ashplant to break Bella Cohen's light fixture, he also shatters light, suggesting lightning. For Wotan in the *Ring* the ash spear means godly authority and powers achieved, while for Stephen it symbolizes his desires and ambition. Thus, the connection with Wotan's spear serves to deflate Stephen's position by contrasting it with the god's.

But there is a second level of Wagnerian allusions that surround Stephen's cane, for he also uses it as a sword. Earlier it was remarked that he calls it his "ash sword." What makes this conclusively a Wagnerian allusion is the fact that he calls it "Nothung" in the Circe chapter. When Stephen breaks Bella Cohen's chandelier with his ashplant, he cries "Nothung." Weldon Thornton, in his *Allusions in Ulysses*, traces this to the *Ring*: "Nothung is the sword of Siegfried in Wagner's *The Ring of the Nibelung*. It first appears in *The Valkyrie*, when Siegmund, the father of Siegfried, draws the sword from the ash tree and names it. . . . Later in this same opera, Wotan intervenes in Siegmund's battle with Hunding to break the sword and give the victory to Hunding. In *Siegfried*, Siegfried himself reforges the sword and slays the dragon Fafner with it. And in *The Dusk of the Gods*, Siegfried sees the sword as the guardian of his trust in his oath (made while under a spell) with Gunther."[13] It should be added here that the sword Nothung was originally placed in the ash tree by Wotan, who told Sieglinde that she would love the man who could draw it out of the tree. Her husband Hunding could not, nor could any other man who attempted it except Siegmund. Thus, in the *Ring*, the sword is always connected with the Wälsungs, first Siegmund, then his son, Siegfried.

When Stephen refers to the *Ring* specifically and significantly on page 560, he strengthens further the connections with Siegfried: "Stephen (Extends his hand to her smiling and chants to the air of the Bloodoath in the *Dusk of the Gods*) Hangende Hunger/ Fragende Frau,/ Macht uns alle kaput." In the first act of *Götterdämmerung* Siegfried and Gunther swear an oath of blood brotherhood on the sword Nothung. Thornton gives the following analysis for this allusion in *Ulysses*: "The air of the blood oath alludes to the scene in Act I of Wagner's *Dusk of the Gods* in which Siegfried and Gunther swear an oath of blood brotherhood. Stephen's lines derive in part . . . from a passage in *The Valkyrie* (Act I, scene ii) in which Siegmund addressed Sieglinde as 'Fragende Frau' (questioning wife). Stephen's whole phrase may be translated 'Unfulfilled longing, a questioning wife, ruin us everyone.'"[14] Although Thornton does give us the facts behind the allusion, he does not explain its function. Basically, what intellectual Stephen is doing here is making a rather esoteric joke by parodying the Wagnerian situation of blood brotherhood in this rank, whorehouse setting. He is also unconsciously connecting himself with Siegmund and Siegfried and their heroic world, thereby sustaining the irony noted earlier. But the connection with Siegfried and Siegmund's sword Nothung is definitely established, for the blood oath in *Götterdämmerung* is sworn on it. By contrast, Stephen's histrionic allusions to Wagnerian operatic myth and music make him look pretentious and preposterous. He can not fit into the molds of either Siegmund or Siegfried; instead, all he can do is turn their words into nonsense. The blood oath in Bella Cohen's brothel in Circe is comically absurd, yet it builds a link with myth and mythic characters. The fact that the motif itself is mentioned also adds a musical dimension to the allusion.

But the most famous Wagnerian allusion in Circe is the "Nothung" episode when Stephen breaks Bella Cohen's light fixture with his ashplant while yelling the name of the famous sword: "Stephen: Nothung! (He lifts his ashplant high with both hands and smashes the chandelier. Time's livid final flame leaps and, in the following darkness, ruin of all space, shattered glass and toppling masonry)" (p. 583). The importance of this allusion to the famous sword is enhanced by the light-and-dark imagery in the passage. Stephen has used his "augur's rod" to create lightning, but not for long, because darkness soon follows. At first glance the act may look heroic and self-assertive, but he has only damaged the room's source of light. The passage does, however, conclusively connect the ashplant with the sword Nothung. The cane has become symbolic of Stephen's own young manhood, his sexual maturity, and, by implication, his phallus. This is also how the sword operates in the *Ring*; it is given by Wotan to his son and grandson, when they are mature, as a means of defending themselves. Edmund Epstein's explanation of the sword is useful: "Stephen's dance is, then, a weapon dance celebrating the acquisition of Nothung, a sword, a symbol of manhood . . . . Stephen's ashplant, his 'augur's rod,' the symbol of his vocation as an artist, is now the third leg of a three-legged dance, and a sword, and a phallus."[15] Epstein discusses the generational conflict in the novel and in these terms the sword represents Stephen's newer generation, which tries to assert its own manhood and sexuality in spite of the older generation's reluctance to relinquish its traditional powers. When Stephen breaks Bella Cohen's chandelier with his cane, he is symbolically asserting his own young manhood.

Epstein explains the aftermath of this climactic action in the following passage: "The first thing that Stephen does after the great apocalypse, after the downfall of the old order and his symbolical accession to maturity, is to rush out into the street in search of a feminine reality for him to fertilize."[16] Here Epstein pushes the analogy too far and becomes insensitive to the passage's mock-epic tone. Stephen's flight is comic and deflating rather than heroic. The anti-heroic quality of his gesture is made especially apparent soon afterwards, when Bella calls for the police: ''Stephen, abandoning his ashplant, his head and arms thrown back stark, beats the ground and flees from the room past the whores at the door'' (p. 583). What hero would abandon his sacred weapon and flee from the enemy? The comparison with Siegfried is a way of mocking Stephen's gesture rather than ennobling it. In the confusion and darkness that ensue, it is Bloom who literally picks up the pieces and tries to deal with the angry Bella. Significantly, he also ''snatches up Stephen's ashplant'' (p. 583). Fatherly, protective Bloom is the true wielder of the augur's rod, and to the end of this chapter it is Bloom who carries it. On the last page of Circe the following highly important stage direction appears: ''He [Stephen] stretches out his arms, sighs again, and curls his body. Bloom holding his hat and ashplant stands erect. A dog barks in the distance. Bloom tightens and loosens his grip on the ashplant. He looks down on Stephen's face and form'' (p. 609). A ritual occurs here and Bloom has become a Wotan-like figure. He has the greater right to carry Wotan's ash spear since he is more mature than Stephen, and he is a representative of the older order. As Stephen takes the foetal position, Bloom is enacting a symbolic fatherhood as well as a benediction. The mighty, lightning-wielding ashplant is at last in its proper position in the hands of Bloom. The ashplant's Wagnerian allusions have served several functions in *Ulysses*: to deflate the proud Stephen, to accrue symbolic import, and to add to the stature of the now godlike Bloom. But perhaps the dog barking in the background in this passage is there to remind us that this is Joycean comedy and not Wagnerian tragedy, lest we take it all too seriously. Joyce's tone very shrewdly allows him to create mythic comedy, and Wagner has helped him.

In Eumaeus the first sentence mentions the ashplant: ''Preparatory to anything else Mr. Bloom brushed off the greater bulk of the shavings and handed Stephen the hat and ashplant and bucked him up generally in orthodox samaritan fashion, which he very badly needed'' (pp. 612-13). After this the cane is never again mentioned, for its symbolical function is over, but it has been very useful to Joyce. Because Stephen's cane suggests both younger and older generations, Joyce cleverly dramatizes the cyclical rather than progressive nature of the conflict. Stephen desires the powers of the older god, yet wants to assert his own authority, thus the conflict is archetypal and will continue. Both Wotan's spear and Siegfried's sword are contained in Stephen's cane, but spear and sword are not reconciled in the *Ring*. When Wotan surrounds his sleeping daughter Brünnhilde with protective magic fire at the end of *Die Walküre*, he says that only the man who is not afraid of his spear will win Brünnhilde. In the second scene of the last act of *Siegfried*, Wotan uses his spear to try to stop the young Siegfried from reaching her, but he breaks Wotan's spear with Nothung. Only then does Wotan step aside and allow him to reach his daughter, saying that he cannot stop him; Wotan thereby fulfills the prophecy he made at the end of *Die Walküre*. Unlike Wagner, Joyce has combined both spear and sword in Stephen's ashplant, and thereby established the cyclical nature of the generational conflict in *Ulysses*.

I have discussed the Wagnerian pattern of a female figure combined with the sea in *Portrait*. This pattern also occurs in *Ulysses* and is established right from the first chapter of the novel, Telemachus. There Stephen thinks of his recently deceased mother and her demands. ``Silently, in a dream she had come to him after her death, her wasted body within its loose brown grave clothes giving off an odour of wetted ashes. Cross the threadbare cuffedge he saw the sea hailed as a great sweet mother by the wellfed voice beside him'' (p. 5). This passage creates an essential connection between Stephen's mother and the sea, just as the fourth chapter of *Portrait* joined female with the sea. Here, however, the sea is a replacement for his real mother, since she is dead.

This pattern also figures prominently in Sirens, the most musical chapter in the novel. Here, too, Wagnerian references and parallels occur, but to the librettos of the operas rather than to the music.

The best discussion I have found of the musical elements in this chapter is Zack Bowen's "The Bronzegold Sirensong: A Musical Analysis of the Sirens Episode in Joyce's *Ulysses*." Bowen begins by destroying the myth that the chapter is really a *fuga per canonem*, started by Joyce himself (probably because he was amused by the credulity of his listeners) and repeated by Stuart Gilbert in his book on *Ulysses*. After examining the chapter musically, Bowen asserts: "If the chapter is not composed along fugal lines, neither is it an opera . . . . If anything, the Sirens chapter is a medley or chronicle of the musical themes of *Ulysses*."[17] After listing and explaining all the musical devices that Joyce employed in the chapter, Bowen ends with the following assertion: "Yet, after seemingly the worse has been done to remove the sentimentality from Bloom's position, a real pathos has been created, and the music has helped to do it . . . . The very profusion of musical imagery centering upon the love and war themes in the chapter gives those themes an epic dimension."[18]

Within the chapter's love theme, which Bowen describes, the Wagnerian pattern of female coupled with water occurs. To substantiate this, here are some sentences from the first page of the chapter: "Bronze by Gold heard the Hoofirons, Steelrining imperthnthn thnthnthn. Chips, picking chips off rocky thumbnail, chips. Horrid! and gold flushed more. A husky fifenote blew. Blew. Blue bloom is on the Gold pinnacles hair . . . . The morn is breaking . . . . A sail! A veil awave upon the waves" (p. 256). The chapter opens with the dawn and mentions gold and water. The two barmaids are often identified by their dark and light hair, or "bronze" and "gold." The appearance of gold, the circumstance of the dawn rising, and the occurrence of water imagery in the opening of the chapter are similar to the opening of the *Ring* tetralogy. The first scene of *Das Rheingold* takes place at the bottom of the Rhine as the dawn breaks, with the Rhinemaidens there to defend their gold, for it gives the river its beauty. When the sun appears, it sends light onto the beautiful gold, which thereby brightens the entire scene. But then the dwarf Alberich appears.

On the second page of Sirens the following passage occurs: "Low in dark middle earth. Embedded ore. Naminedamine. All gone. All fallen. Tiny, her tremulous fernfoils of maindenhair. Amen! He gnashed in fury. Fro. To, fro. A baton cool protruding. Bronzelydia by Minagold. By bronze, by gold in oceangreen of shadow. Bloom. Old Bloom" (p. 257). This ominous entrance for Bloom parallels Alberich's appearance in the first scene of *Das Rheingold*. "Low in middle earth" connects with the dwarf's origin as a miner, while "he gnashed in fury" is a perfect description of Alberich in the first scene of the opera. What infuriates him into stealing the gold is the fact that the Rhinemaidens tease him heartlessly. "Oceangreen of shadow" establishes a sea referent for this chapter and the water is consistently connected with the barmaids, who enjoy teasing most of their customers, especially Bloom. The Wagnerian combination of water and woman is operating here and the whole chapter floats on this pattern, while Joyce's barmaids are very similar to Wagner's Rhinemaidens.

In Sirens the Rhinemaidens are, comically, really just barmaids at the Ormond Bar, but they share many characteristics with Wagner's river sprites, for both are teases who enjoy laughing at men and their sexual desires. The Rhinemaidens taunt Alberich when he tries to capture their attention. They also appear in Act III, scene i of *Götterdämmerung* and try to get their gold back from Siegfried, who is wearing it as a ring. When he first refuses, they laugh at him for being such a miser and conclude that his wife must beat him. The barmaids at the Ormond Bar, Lydia Douce and Mina Kennedy,[19] are very aware of all the men in the bar and the sexual goings-on of Blazes Boylan and several of the others. The following passage illustrates the girls' teasing quality, (and also emphasizes the "goldness" of one of them): "She laughed,—O Wept! Aren't men frightful idiots? . . . In a giggling peal young gold-bronze voices blended, Douce with Kennedy your other eye. They threw young heads back, bronze gigglegold, to let freefly their laughter, screaming, your other, signals to each other, high piercing notes . . . . O greasy eyes! Imagine being married to a man bottom of the Rhine just before dawn and *Die Götterdämmerung* ends with the Rhine overflowing during predawn darkness. The primordial innocence of the world has been reestablished by the end of the opera and the gold is back where it belongs, in the river with the Rhinemaidens. Its luster gives the undulating river its beauty, and only there does it do any good for the world. The high point of the *Ring*, the last scene of *Siegfreid* when Brünnhilde and Siegfried are first in love, is reflected in the bright sunshine Wagner puts in his stage directions. *The Waves* is structured similarly, with high noon for the central section of the novel. The artistic effect of this circular structure is similar in both works. The cyclical nature of existence, with a suggestion of life after death, is a major implication of this form. Also the waving, rhythmic movement of water is used to emphasize the concepts of fertility and circular movement. This circularity is reinforced in Wagner's tetralogy by the central symbol of the work, for the ring itself is, of course, a circle.

Woolf's *The Waves* also contains a pattern of rings. The rings in this novel are both visual and aural and first appear, significantly, after the italicized section of the first chapter. The sun has just appeared over the sea and the first line after the description is: "'I see a ring,' said Bernard, 'hanging above me. It quivers and hangs in a loop of light'" (p. 180). This begins a whole series of images of rings, circles, and loops. Soon afterwards Louis talks of his efforts to "forge a ring of steel" (p. 201), as he calls his attempts to write poetry. Several pages later Rhoda sees Miss Lambert and notices: "She lets her tasselled silken cloak slip down, and only her purple ring still glows, her vinous, but amethystine ring" (p. 205). Bernard often makes smoke rings while he thinks: "A smoke ring issues from my lips . . . and circles him, bringing him into contact" (p. 221). Louis uses the word when he comments about a book he is reading: "It contains some forged rings, some perfect statements, a few words, but poetry" (p. 240). The form suggests security and stability to Rhoda; and at one point when she is afraid, she says: "The circle is destroyed. We are thrown asunder" (p.

274). Louis describes his attitude to writing poetry in the following terms: "I shall assemble a few words and forge round us a hammered ring of beaten steel" (p. 292). Once again the ring of steel is seen as an ordering principle for art. Susan uses the image aurally to describe her happiness on her farm: "When the lark peals high his ring of sound and it falls through the air like an apple paring, I stoop" (p. 294). During Bernard's final monologue he says: "There was no past, no future; merely the moment in its ring of light, and our bodies; and the inevitable climax, the ecstasy" (p. 351). This crucial sentence summarizes the novel's cyclical theme. Bernard makes the same point toward the end of his final monologue when he says: "Tuesday follows Monday; Wednesday, Tuesday. Each spreads the same ripple. The being grows rings, like a tree. Like a tree, leaves fall" (p. 373). The rings of a tree suggest the whole circular process of growth and death that Woolf is trying to portray. All of the characters mention a ring during the novel and the image is consistently used to imply an order in both life and art. Rings of steel, rings of gold, a ringing sound, even smoke rings—Woolf uses them all to make her point symbolically. Wagner's golden ring, as we have seen, also suggests the repeated rhythm of life and death, but he uses it for other things as well—accursed greed, material possessions, and Siegfried's love for Brünnhilde when he gives her the ring as a marriage gift in the first act of *Götterdämmerung*. But one basic meaning of a ring, its circular form symbolizing a circular concept of life's progression, is used in both *The Waves* and the *Ring*.

Another cluster of Wagnerian references, coming from *Parsifal*, emerges in the novel. As Blissett has pointed out, the name "Percival" is a variant of "Parsifal."[14] We know from Woolf's "Impressions at Bayreuth" that she was very fond of this opera, raising again the possibility of an influence. Wagner's Parsifal is based upon a fabled knight from the medieval Grail legends of Eschenbach. Woolf's Percival also assumes mythic stature, partially because he is always viewed tangentially, through the other characters and by his effect upon them. Early in the novel Louis like that, she cried. With his bit of beard!'' (pp. 257-60). This could certainly be Wagner's baiting Rhinemaidens. Here they are laughing at Bloom, which makes him the Alberich-figure in the Wagnerian parallel.

Another significant passage, which solidifies this connection, occurs in the following excerpt: ''They pined in depth of ocean shadow, gold by beerpull, bronze by maraschino . . . . Only the harp. Lovely gold glowering light . . . . Golden ship'' (pp. 269-71). The harp, music, light, and water are prominent here, in addition to the gold. The water imagery is also sustained by the fact that Lydia Douce has brought a seashell to the bar from her recent vacation. The following passage mentions it: ''Bloom through the bardoor saw a shell held at their ears. He heard more faintly that they heard, each of herself, alone, then each for other, hearing the plash of waves . . . . Been to the seaside. Lovely seaside girls'' (p. 281). It sometimes seems that the Ormond Bar is at the bottom of the sea, with all the water that is mentioned. The water imagery, the emphasis upon the gold, the opening at dawn, the suggestions of Bloom as Alberich, and finally the personalities of Joyce's Ormond barmaids—all have specific parallels in Wagner's opera. This pattern of allusions serves to buttress the epic qualities of the chapter, as well as adding comedy to much of the action. Joyce's unique combination of comedy and myth gives the chapter an epic dimension—more specifically, mock-epic. The combination of water and woman, unlike the earlier reference to Stephen's dead mother, cleverly links myth with comedy.

The union of water and woman also occurs in the Nausicaa section of *Ulysses*. The first paragraph of this episode ends with a description of a vespers service: '' . . . on the quiet church whence there streamed forth at times upon the stillness the voice of prayer to her who is in her pure radiance a beacon ever to the storm-tossed heart of man, Mary, star of the sea'' (p. 346). The ''fine writing'' quality of the prose tells the reader that Joycean parody is afoot; this chapter satirizes Gerty MacDowell's sentimental approach to life. But behind her description of events in the chapter there are repeated references to the church service and its litany to "Mary, star of the sea." Several times throughout this chapter Mary, a Christian archetype of womanly comfort, and her worshipers are mentioned, and they finally provide a comic background to the masturbation scene. The name "Mary" is itself a variant of the Latin *mare*, or sea. This combination of woman with the sea is another comic aspect of the Wagnerian pattern we have been noticing. Joyce enjoyed satirizing Irish Catholicism in this novel, and here Mariolatry is the target.

The final chapter in *Ulysses* contains its last manifestation of this woman/water pattern. Molly Bloom's soliloquy contains several important references to water, which imply something about her function in the novel. The water references occur most frequently toward the end of the soliloquy, when she thinks more of sex. On page 765 she says: "The smell of the sea excited me of course." Molly would be very aware of the sea and its smell because she was raised on Gibraltar. Toward the end of the chapter, when she begins to think of nature, she says: "God of heaven theres nothing like nature the wild mountains then the sea and the waves rushing" (p. 781). The connection of water with Molly's sexuality is made most explicit on the last two pages of the novel. When she recalls first making love with Bloom, she reminisces: "Leading him on till he asked me to say yes and I wouldnt answer first only looked out over the sea" (p. 782). Finally, on the last page and just before she remembers her decision to make love the first time, she says: "And O that awful deepdown torrent O and the sea crimson sometimes like fire" (p. 783). Her repeated references to water suggest her own sexuality and parallel Wagnerian water imagery. While this pattern also exists in *Ulysses*, its connection with Wagner is weakest in this last chapter, for by the end of the novel it has become almost purely Joycean.

Two topics so far in *Ulysses*—the Wagnerian allusions that surround Stephen's ashplant and the juxtaposition of woman and water—also existed in a simpler form in *Portrait*. The final Wagnerian pattern in Ulysses does not appear in any of Joyce's earlier fiction. Only in this novel are there repeated references to Wagner's *Der Fliegende Holländer*. Many of the allusions refer specifically to the Wagnerian version of the ancient myth, which reinforces the connection with the composer. The Proteus chapter ends with the following paragraph: "He turned his face over a shoulder, rere regardant. Moving through the air high spars of a three-master, her sails brailed up on the crosstrees, homing, upstream, silently moving, a slient ship" (p. 51). This mysterious "silently moving, a silent ship" that Stephen sees is the first appearance of a pattern that suggests the Flying Dutchman. Such a pattern operates as a more nautical parallel to the Homeric references in *Ulysses*.

This pattern also occurs in Circe. Bloom alludes twice to the Flying Dutchman myth, and both allusions occur during his fantasized vision of himself as Lord Mayor of Dublin: "Bloom: (in Alderman's gown and chain) Electors of Arran Quay, Inns Quay, Rotunda, Mountjoy and North Dock, better run a tramline, I say, from the cattlemarket to the river. That's the music of the future. That's my programme. *Cui Bono?* But our buccaneering Vanderdeckens in their phantom ship of finance . . . . (Impassionately) These flying Dutchmen or lying Dutchmen as they recline in their upholstered poop, casting dice, what reck they . . . . The poor man starves while they are grassing their royal mountain stags or shooting peasants and Phartridges in their purblind pomp pelp and power" (pp. 478-79). Vanderdecken, the captain of the Flying Dutchman, is mentioned specifically here. "The music of the future" refers to Wagner's famous use of the phrase, which establishes the reference as Wagnerian rather than just mythic. Bloom connects the myth with the inequities of capitalism and defends the rights of oppressed workers. But the spelling and vocabulary in this passage remind us that this is a dream-vision and the resultant effect is farcically mythic, yet a serious intent is also present.

The chapter with the most allusions to *Der Fliegende Holländer* is Eumaeus, where the old sailor becomes a comic parallel to the wandering Dutchman. The fact that the sailor says he has not seen his "own true wife" (p. 624) for seven years parallels the Dutchman myth. This pattern is also similar to the wandering of the hero in the Odyssey, but the repeated references to the ocean and the sailor fit the Dutchman myth more exactly. Another reference in Eumaeus that is more specifically Wagnerian occurs in the following passage: "However, reverting to friend Sinbad and his horrifying adventures (who reminded him a bit of Ludwig, *alias* Ledwidge, when he occupied the boards of the Gaiety when Michael Gunn was identified with the management in *The Flying Dutchman*, a stupendous success, and his host of admirers came in large numbers, everyone simply flocking to hear him . . .)" (p. 636). Why Wagner's *Flying Dutchman*, of all operas? The reference is part of a pattern of allusions to the sea, the old sailor who tells the highly improbable stories, and the myth of Vanderdecken. On the next page the pattern is sustained: "Interest, however, was starting to flag somewhat all round and the others got on to talking about accidents at sea, ships lost in a fog, collisions with icebergs, all that sort of thing. Shipahoy, of course, had his own say to say. He had doubled the Cape a few odd times and weathered a monsoon, a kind of wind, in the China sea" (pp. 637-38). The sailor has become comically mythic, a "shipahoy" type who exaggerates about wandering at sea. In the guise of the captain of the Flying Dutchman, he is part of a series of allusions to Wagner's sea captain. This pattern supports the wandering Odysseus motif in the novel, but it provides a more nautical atmosphere of ships, sailors, the sea, and the search for a fruitful woman.

A. Walton Litz has said of the novel: "*Ulysses* belongs to many different traditions, one of which is the tradition of the Wagnerian novel, another that of the Symbolist poets who tried to fuse musical and poetic effects."[20] As we have seen, however, the Wagnerian materials in *Ulysses* depend primarily on the operas' librettos, although the music is mentioned on several occasions. Wagnerian opera has provided Joyce with a means of combining comedy with myth in his epic of an Irish Everyman, *Ulysses*.

In *Finnegans Wake* the aspect of Wagnerism most frequently

noticed by the critics is its extensive use of leitmotifs. Litz mentions Joyce's debt to Wagnerian structuring for the form of *Finnegans Wake*.[21] Clive Hart also discusses the Wagnerian leitmotif and Joyce's extensive use of it in the *Wake*.[22] But Wagnerian patterns also occur that form meaningful wholes and help Joyce add a comically mythic dimension to his novel. In both *Portrait* and *Ulysses* the combination of the female principle with water was noticed and it was pointed out that this is also a recurrent pattern in Wagner's operas; this pattern also exists in *Finnegans Wake*. By the end of the novel Anna Livia Plurabelle becomes the river Liffey in her husband's sleeping mind and returns to her father, the ocean, for death and rebirth. Ultimately, her totality includes her daughter Isobel and all women; she is an earth-mother figure, although river-mother would be more precise. This pattern helps Joyce to make Anna both a real character and an archetypal life force. However, by the time that Joyce wrote *Finnegans Wake*, he had used this pattern often enough that it became completely his own and lost its Wagnerian references.

But a cluster of references in the *Wake* is generated from Wagner's *Tristan und Isolde*. There are many versions of this myth; David Hayman, however, who has written an excellent article on Joyce's sources for it, reports that Wagner's version is the principal source. Joyce himself had a long interest in the story, partially because of its Celtic origin. We have seen him use it in a story from *The Dubliners*, "A Painful Case." His play *Exiles* also uses the theme of the cuckolded husband through submerged references to Tristan and King Mark. Finnegan, the dreaming tavern keeper, lives in Chapelizod like Mr. Duffy in "A Painful Case." This town is, according to the myth, the home of Isolde. Finnegan's daughter is named Isobel, which is a variant of "Isolde." Finnegan has incestuous feelings toward her, and sometimes thinks of himself as King Mark to her Isolde. The character of "Mildew Lisa" keeps reappearing in the novel; the name is a parody of the first line of the *Liebestod* from *Tristan*, *"Mild und leise*." Such specifically Wagnerian allusions as these, which prove conclusively that Wagner's version of the myth was the one used, add mythic and archetypal dimensions to the novel. The Wagnerian patterns are a means of establishing Finnegan as a repository of Western myth and an archetypal everyman.

David Hayman describes the structural functions of the allusions to *Tristan* in the following passage: "In *Finnegans Wake* the tale of Tristan and Isolde functions as a theme, that is, as a variable complex of recognizable motifs contributing along with a number of other themes to the book's formal unity. Though Joyce never presents his version of the tale fully or consecutively, he does through the medium of strategically placed passages suggest a Tristan subplot paralleling the book's major plot: the decline and fall and the re-instatement of the everyman hero HCE."[23] The addition of *Tristan* allusions to the major plot adds more mythic elements to the *Wake*. While recounting the young Joyce's early fondness for Wagner's *Tristan and Isolde*, Hayman mentions aspects of it that also appear in the *Wake*: "Wagner's version, the only version of the tale with which the young writer was thoroughly familiar, emphasizes, in addition to the Celtic milieu, several themes to which biographical evidence demonstrates Joyce's emotional commitment in 1913: exile, brotherly love and brotherly betrayal, envy, adultery and the half-willing cuckold, and mystical and magical as opposed to legal and religious possession of the beloved."[24] As Hayman points out, these themes also appear in *Finnegans Wake*.

The single Wagnerian phrase that is repeated most frequently in the *Wake* is the pun on the first line of the *Liebestod*, "Mildew Lisa." Adaline Glasheen, in her *Census of Finnegans Wake*, lists at least twelve appearances of this name in the novel,[25] under its normal spelling and variants like "Meldundleize"[26] and "Formalisa Loves deathhow." An understanding of the function of this character in the novel will further our comprehension of the Wagnerian pun. Glasheen lists "Mildew Lisa" as one of the variant names for: "Issy, Izzy, Isabel, Isolde—daughter of Anna Livia and HCE."[27] She also describes this character: "Issy melts into all the temptresses in FW. She is the desire that lures her father, HCE—lures every man—up the dark, dream garden path."[28] Why, then, would Joyce sometimes refer to her as "Mildew Lisa"?

*Tristan und Isolde* ends with Isolde's famous final monologue, the *Liebestod*. She sings this over the corpse of Tristan, who has just died, but she describes a hallucination. Despite the fact that she is standing by his corpse, she envisions him as smiling, alive, happy, and beckoning to her. The scene summarizes the opera's theme of love and death, for onstage the audience sees the corpse of Tristan but hears Isolde's assertion that he is alive and their love is triumphant at last. It should be added that Isolde herself has been presented in the first act of the opera as the quintessential temptress. Tristan tries to avoid her then, but she demands that he come to her and offers him what she thinks is the death potion; however, her maid Brangaene has instead given her the love potion. Her position as temptress in the first act of the opera is certainly parallel to Joyce's Issy, a connection that gives that character mythic significance. But in the *Wake* she is often called "Mildew Lisa," which connects her with Isolde's final vision of love and death during the *Liebestod*. The cycle of love and death is a corollary of the recurring cycles of life, death, and rebirth in the novel. Just as the last sentence of the *Wake* runs into its first, and ALP flows into death and rebirth by seeking her father, the ocean, at the end of the novel, the phrase *Mildew Lisa* serves to remind the reader of the cycle of love and death. The primordial temptress, Issy, is part of a basic rhythm in the book and Joyce reminds us of this through his Wagnerian pun, "Mildew Lisa." Of course, there is an element of parody here as well, for the novel is essentially a comic work. The first line of the *Liebestod*, then, has provided Joyce with a clever device for combining comedy with myth.

We have noticed Joyce's use of *Der Fliegende Holländer* in *Ulysses*, and it also appear in the *Wake* for a similar effect. Finnegan, like Bloom, is a wanderer, although by night in dreams rather than by day. Vanderdecken, the Dutch seaman, Senta, and

Eric, the hunter who also loves her, all appear in the *Wake* through buried and distorted references to their names and story. The attractive Senta is the first to arrive, in a clever parenthetical aside: "(ringrang, the chimes of sex appealing as conchitas with sentas stray, rung!)" (p. 268, ll. 2,3). Then Eric makes a brief entry: "While they either took a heft. Or the other swore his eric. Heaved two, spluiced the menbrace" (p. 316, ll. 8, 9). Soon afterwards the Dutchman himself appears: " . . . the bugganeering wanderducken, he sazd, (that his pumps may ship awhoyle . . . how you was, Ship Alouset?)" (p. 323, ll. 1-4). Vanderdecken's success with Senta, and this despite Eric, gets an earthy retelling by the end of the *Wake*: "Roof Seckesign van der Deckel and get her story from him! Recall Sickerson, the lizzyboy! Seckersen, magnon of Errick! . . . High liquor made lust torpid dough hunt her orchid. Hunt her orchid! Gob and he fount it right enough! With her shoes upon his shoulders" (p. 530, ll. 20-25). Once again comedy, here of a particularly lusty variety, is created from Wagnerian myth. Rather than redemption through love, here the Dutchman simply makes drunken love to his Senta.

A final group of Wagnerian puns in the *Wake* clusters around the composer's life, his theater at Bayreuth, and his operas' titles. Joyce's youthful Wagnerism had waned quite a bit by the late 20s and 30s. The generally anti-Wagnerian sentiment among intellectuals and writers in these decades was, in part, shared by Joyce. As a result, the Wagnerian puns in the *Wake* tend to poke fun at the German composer. "Wagoner would his mudheeldy wheesindonk" (p. 230, l. 12) is a reference to Wagner's famous love affair with Mathilde von Wesendonk, and her name becomes debased for ironic effect. The phrase "dedder wagoners, pullars off societies" (p. 540, l. 24) comments sarcastically on Wagner's grandiose plans for a new German society. This same ironic point is made in the phrase "humanity's fahrman by societyleader, voguener" (p. 577, l. 13). By the 30s, Joyce could witness firsthand what some of Wagner's social theories could lead to, hence his sarcasm. One of Wagner's major means of reforming German society was through definitive productions of his music-dreams in his personally designed theater at Bayreuth. In the 30s, while Joyce was working on *Finnegans Wake*, Hitler (with the help of Winifred Wagner, the widow of the composer's son) converted the theater into a center for Nazi propaganda. Joyce's response to this is reflected in his alterations of "Bayreuth" in the *Wake*, where it becomes "Boyrut" (p. 229, l. 34) and "Bayroyt" (p. 500, l. 24). Toward the end of the novel the following sentence occurs: "It is often quite guttergloomering in our duol and gives Wankyrious thoughts to the head but the banders of the pentapolitan poleetsfurceers bassoons into it on windy wodensday, their well booming wolvertones, Ulvos! Ulvos!" (p. 565, ll. 2-5). In addition to comically punning on Wagnerian titles like *Götterdämmerung* and *Walküre*, the passage also refers disparagingly to Wagner's well-known predilection for the brass in his orchestration. Joyce's use of Wagnerian patterns in *Finnegans Wake*, then, covers a broad spectrum that includes both mythic elevation, comic punning, and parody.

Wagnerian patterns exist in all of Joyce's major works. While the mature Joyce was not too affected by Wagner's music, he always remained interested in the operas as mythic dramas. His fiction indicates an increasing use of Wagnerian patterns for a variety of artistic effects. In "A Painful Case" we found Joyce's first use of Wagnerian material, *Tristan und Isolde*. The references to the opera in that story comment ironically on the sterility of Mr. Duffy and his cautious refusal of Mrs. Sinico's offer of love. In *A Portrait of the Artist as a Young Man* we noticed Dixon's use of the forest-bird motif from *Siegfried* and its function in the novel. Also, Stephen's ashplant in that novel is a reference to Wagner's Wotan and the spear he carries and thereby dramatizes Stephen's pretentious desire for power and authority. Also, in *Portrait*, the fourth chapter ends with a vision of woman and water, which is the first of an important series of such allusions in Joyce's fiction. In *Ulysses* the ashplant cane that Stephen carries also has Wagnerian overtones, but they are used in a more complex way. In addition to the reference to Wotan's spear, which we saw in *Portrait*, a new pattern of allusions to Siegmund and Siegfried's sword Nothung also appears. They suggest Stephen's desire for a means of defense to assert his own generation and his own sexuality; the sword is a phallic symbol of his young manhood. The fact that the ashplant refers to both Wotan's spear and Siegfried's sword helps Joyce imply that the novel's generational conflict is cyclical rather than progressive. *Ulysses* also employs the symbolical combination of water and the female principle: in Stephen's vision of his mother as the sea, in the Rhinemaiden allusions in Sirens, in "Mary, star of the sea" of Nausicaa, and finally in the water imagery in Molly Bloom's final soliloquy. Joyce shared Wagner's redemptive view of woman; the symbolical connection of woman with the fertility of water exemplifies this. Also in *Ulysses*, a pattern of allusions to *Der Fliegende Holländer* provides the novel with a nautical counterpart to Homer's Odyssey myth. These allusions help Joyce to characterize Bloom's sympathy with the sufferings of the ordinary man and portray the old sailor in Eumaeus as an archetypal teller of tall sea-tales. Finally, in *Finnegans Wake*, the symbolic combination of water with the female principle figures prominently. We have also seen how *Tristan und Isolde* provides a mythic body of allusions to the *Wake* that helps Joyce to structure the novel and parody the Tristan myth. But in the process his characters, by their connection with the characters in the opera, have become more mythic. This is especially true of "Mildew Lisa," a name used for HCE's daughter. The Wagnerian pun involved is comic, but it also reminds the reader of the cycle of love and death. The *Flying Dutchman* myth, also alluded to in the novel, becomes a source of comic parody. The *Wake* also contains many other puns—on Wagner's life and theater—and titles that cleverly parody Wagnerolatry. Joyce used Wagnerian patterns for many effects in his fiction, from mythic elevation to mythic parody; but the effect that recurs most frequently is comedy, which includes various shades of subtlety from irony to punning wordplay.

## Notes

1. Richard Ellman, *James Joyce* (New York, 1959), pp. 156-58.
2. James Joyce, *The Critical Writings of James Joyce* (New York, 1959), pp. 40-41.
3. Ibid., p. 43.
4. Ibid., pp. 75-76.
5. James Joyce, *Letters of James Joyce* (New York, 1957), 2:25. Hereafter referred to in ths text.
6. Ellmann, p. 473.
7. Ibid., p. 116.
8. Ibid., p. 393.
9. Edouard Dujardin, *Le Monologue Interieur: Son Apparitions, Ses Origines, Sa Place dans l'Oeuvre de James Joyce* (Paris, 1931), pp. 37-40.
10. William Blissett, "James Joyce in the Smithy of His Soul," in *James Joyce Today*, ed. Thomas F. Staley (Bloomington, Ind., 1966), p. 133.
11. James Joyce, *A Portrait of the Artist as a Young Man* (New York, 1967), p. 237 Hereafter referred to in the text.
12. James Joyce, *Ulysses* (New York, 1961), p. 37. Hereafter referred to in the text.
13. Weldon Thorton, *Allusions in Ulysses* (Chapel Hill, N.C., 1961), p. 418.
14. Ibid., p. 410.
15. Edmund L. Epstein, *The Ordeal of Stephen Dedalus: The Conflict of the Generations in James Joyce's A Portrait of the Artist as a Young Man* (Carbondale, Ill., 1971), p. 163.
16. Ibid., p. 172.
17. Zack Bowen, "The Bronzegold Sirensong: A Musical Analysis of the Sirens Episode in Joyce's *Ulysses*," in *Literary Monographs*, ed. Eric Rothstein and Thomas K. Dunseath (Madison, Wis., 1967), pp. 249-50.
18. Ibid., p. 297.
19. Wagner's first wife was also named Mina. A hint, perhaps.
20. A. Walton Litz, *The Art of James Joyce: Method and Design in Ulysses and Finnegans Wake* (London, 1961), p. 64.
21. Ibid., pp. 64-65.
22. Clive Hart, *Structure and Motif in Finnegans Wake* (Evanston, Ill., 1962), pp. 166-67.
23. David Hayman, "Tristan and Isolde in *Finnegans Wake*: A Study of the Sources and Evolution of a Theme," *Comparative Literature Studies* 1 (1964):93.
24. Ibid., pp. 95-96.
25. Adaline Glasheen, *A Second Census of Finnegans Wake: An Index of the Characters and their Roles* (Evanston, Ill., 1963), p. 150.
26. James Joyce, *Finnegans Wake* (New York, 1971), p. 18, l. 2. Hereafter referred to in the text.
27. Glasheen, *A Second Census*, p. 124.
28. Ibid.

# Conclusion

As this study of Wagnerian patterns in the five authors discussed comes to an end, the question of the place of the influence in the individual writer's whole body of work naturally arises. The focus has been on an individual aspect of five major writers' fiction, but how does this particular aspect look from a broader and longer perspective? We have seen that Conrad used Wagnerian patterns in works that cover a wide period of his writing career. The mythic atmosphere that we have seen him so often strive for was a basic part of his style and theme as a novelist and it recurs in many, but of course not all, of his stories and novels. There are other kinds of novels and stories he wrote, for example, the political novels like *The Secret Agent* and *Under Western Eyes*, and in these works Wagnerian patterns and references do not occur. But, significantly, Conrad does use these patterns in two of his major novels, *Nostromo* and *Victory*.

In D. H. Lawrence's fiction Wagnerian patterns are primarily a phenomenon of his early period, before World War I. Some of his writing after the war also contains vaguely Wagnerian themes like love and death, but by then they are completely Lawrentian and lose their Wagnerian allusions. However, while Lawrence lost most of his interest in Wagner by the time of his full maturity, Wagner did affect one of his major novels, *Women in Love*.

In his tendency to see his dramatic situations in terms of myth, Lawrence turned to Wagner's operas for examples during his early period. But after World War I, when he renounced England and Nordic culture in general, he went to Australia, Mexico, and America for non-European myths as material for his fiction. During the period of his interest in European myth, though, some of Wagner's themes became central to his work.

E. M. Forster, however, uses Wagner in a very different way from the other four writers. For him Wagner was a master of construction, especially with his technique of using three long acts joined together with recurrent patterns of leitmotifs, a method Forster used in many of his novels. The leitmotif itself was a structural model for Forster and his means of solving a major problem with the episodic novel, a unifying form. All Forster's novels except *Maurice* use Wagner's technique, but *Howards End* and *A Passage to India* are most subtle in their uses of leitmotif. In these novels Forster used the technique for his most complex constructions. Direct Wagnerian allusions also occur in many of Forster's short stories and novels, as has been pointed out earlier, but his major method of using Wagner was very different from that of the four other authors discussed.

Of the five novelists, Virginia Woolf's interest in Wagnerian patterns is the most difficult to describe. She was the least obviously influenced by the German composer; yet Wagnerian allusions occur in much of her fiction, starting with the early *The Voyage Out* and extending to the late *The Years*. The Wagnerian allusions in the novels often take on important functions in her characterization. While critics tend to see her as a novelist who strove for realistic characters, we have seen that mythic characters were also one of her interests and here Wagner's operas helped her. But certainly her interest in myth was never so total and all-encompassing as Lawrence's or Joyce's. Woolf was more immediately concerned with the reaction of ordinary people to the potentially mythic personality. Her presentation of mythic figures like Jacob or Percival is accomplished obliquely by their absences and death, rather than through any direct means, and it is here that Wagnerian patterns helped her most significantly.

Joyce's early enthusiasm for Wagner's operas soon waned after he saw many performances of them in Italy, as his correspondence indicates. Although his musical tastes became primarily Italianate, Wagner's music-dramas were one of his lifelong interests. Allusions to them occur in all his novels, but most significantly in *Ulysses* and *Finnegans Wake*. We have seen him use them to support some of the major themes in these novels to give them greater mythic overtones. Yet Joyce the comedian also found in Wagnerian operatics a body ripe for parody and he taps this vein especially well in *Finnegans Wake*, where Wagnerian punning becomes one of the delights of that work. Thematically, Wagnerian patterns also helped Joyce to convey some of the major concerns of his fiction, like the generational conflict, love, incest, and death. But by the time he began work on *Finnegans Wake*, his anti-Wagner feelings were most prominent and the delightful anti-Wagnerian puns in that work add to its comedy.

Although all five of these authors used Wagnerian patterns for various purposes, they were amazingly consistent in the operas they used: *Tristan und Isolde* (most frequently), *Der Ring des Nibelungen, Parsifal,* and *Der Fliegende Holländer*. Why these operas? Why not *Lohengrin, Tannhäuser,* or *Die Meistersinger*? Of the operas used, all but one are Wagner's "pagan" operas. Except for the vaguely Christian *Parsifal*, all the others are either set in pre-Christian times or are totally un-Christian in their characterizations. Of the others, *Tannhäuser* and *Lohengrin* are centrally Christian and their basic conflicts concern Christian as opposed to pagan values. *Die Meistersinger*, Wagner's popular comedy set in the German Renaissance, is his most nationalistic opera. In addition to Christian elements, another marked characteristic of these operas is their popularity among the more old-fashioned Victorian and Edwardian writers. Among the older generation of Edwardian novelists, *Tannhäuser* was the most frequently used Wagnerian opera. Its theme of sacred versus profane love was especially appealing to George Moore, Arnold Bennett, and Oscar Wilde, as we have seen in the Introduction. The five writers we have been studying undoubtedly turned away from these operas because of their excessive popularity among an earlier generation of English novelists and because of their lack of interest in Christian themes. However, there is a notable exception to this generalization, as with all generalizations. *Tristan und Isolde*, though a "pagan" opera, was appealing to both groups of writers.

The Wagnerian opera that Conrad, Lawrence, Woolf, and Joyce referred to most was *Tristan*. Its first act is famous for its psychological studies of the two major characters, and the minor ones are interesting as well. For example, Joyce found the portrait of the maid Brangaene a perfect example of Celtic envy. The first act uses a basic dichotomy of love and hate by portraying Isolde's love so mixed with hatred that she is determined to kill Tristan. The second and third acts contain the famous love and death combination, culminating in the *Liebestod*, and we have seen how influential this was on Conrad, Lawrence, Woolf, and Joyce. The intensely ambivalent portrayal of love is one of the elements in the opera that most attracted them. That this kind of love becomes fated to destruction was especially attractive to Conrad and Lawrence, both of whom found here a modern equivalent for the Greek concept of fate. Joyce was also interested in the incestuous nature of King Marke's love for the young Isolde.

*Der Ring des Nibelungen* was also used by all these writers in varying degrees and with various subtleties. The *Ring*'s huge, epic scope and themes of love, power, and anti-materialism were attractive to these writers, especially Conrad. E. M. Forster used the image of the rainbow bridge several times in his fiction. The concept of redemption through love was close to Lawrence, as has been shown, and this element in the *Ring* undoubtedly appealed to him. The very size and scope of the tetralogy were bound to fascinate any fiction writer interested in epic or mythic effects. The universe of the *Ring* is also pre-Christian and while Christian values, like love, can be imposed on it, its vision is generally mythic and not specifically Christian. Its generational conflict was appealing to Joyce, as we have seen, but all five of these writers were influenced by this vast Wagnerian tetralogy in some way. Here Wagner used the leitmotif most subtly, and Forster knew these scores well.

*Parsifal* was especially alluring to Conrad, Forster, and Woolf. They found its themes of the young innocent and the sacrificial victim appealing and consistent with their own concerns, and the opera provided them with an example of a mythic treatment of the theme of the scapegoat. During the turn of the century *Parsifal* was the least accessible of the operas, since Wagner wanted it performed only at Bayreuth. It was not until the copyright had run out that it was finally staged in London, in 1914. Since it was available only at Bayreuth until then, this opera did not influence all of the writers discussed. From what we know of their respective biographies, E. M. Forster and Virginia Woolf were the only ones of the five who went to Bayreuth, and of them Woolf used *Parsifal* most. The probable explanation is that she knew that opera well enough to allude to it frequently. Conrad also used patterns from *Parsifal*, but while Woolf was interested only in its hero, Conrad was also fascinated by the opera's primordial temptress. Kundry-figures appear in several of Conrad's tales, complete with their magic gardens.

The nautical Joseph Conrad was naturally attracted to Wagner's opera of the sea, *Der Fliegende Holländer*. He was undoubtedly familiar with the myth, but his use of it entailed details that come from Wagner's operatic version. Its themes of the might and power of the sea, its effect upon humanity, the death-wish, and human solitude struck very responsive chords in Conrad. These themes appear in much of his fiction, even apart from the Wagnerian patterns. Conrad also found the concept of redemption through woman appealing and he used it in some of his fiction, although entrapment by woman appears just as frequently. Joyce also used allusions to *Der Fliegende Holländer* in *Ulysses* and *Finnegans Wake*, but often in a subsidiary way to support some of his major themes.

The myths that Wagner made popular in his operas influenced Conrad, Lawrence, Forster, Woolf, and Joyce in varying degrees. For some of them Wagner was primarily a youthful phase of interest in the then avant-garde composer, but for others his work was a lifelong obsession that was especially tied to his librettos and myths. Though some of these writers were much interested in Wagner's music and construction, the element that most generally appealed was Wagnerian mythology. However, Wagner's influence extended to the creation of musical as well as mythic effects in modern fiction. Forster innovated the use of repetitions of leitmotifs for rhythmic effects. I have also discussed the prose of Conrad's novels, with its musical descriptions, especially of the sea. Lawrence's *The Trespasser* is certainly a musical novel, primarily because of the many passages from Wagnerian opera that his major characters are often singing. Wagner's music is played in *The Longest Journey*, and used most dramatically for Agnes's entrance. Rachel Vinrace in Woolf's *The Voyage Out* often plays *Tristan und Isolde*. Stephen Dedalus sings bits of *Die Walküre* and *Götterdämmerung* in *Ulysses*, that most musical of Joyce's works. Wagnerian opera provided these authors with techniques, and of course a vast body of great music, to add musical dimensions to their fiction. Those most antagonistic of the arts, music and literature, were harmoniously joined in some great modern literature through the rainbow bridge of Wagnerian patterns.

# Bibliography

## Primary Sources


Conrad, Joseph. *Almayer's Folly*. Garden City, N.Y.: Doubleday, Page, & Co., 1920.

———. *Chance, A Tale in Two Parts*. Garden City, N.Y.: Doubleday, 1921.

———. *Lettres de Joseph Conrad à Marguerite Poradowska*. Edited by René Rapin. Geneva: Libraire Droaz, 1966.

———. *Letters to William Blackwood and David S. Meldrum*. Edited by William Blackburn. Durham, N.C.: Duke University Press, 1958.

———. *The Nigger of the "Narcissus," A Tale of the Sea*. Garden City, N.Y.: Doubleday, 1920.

———. *Nostromo*. Garden City, N.Y.: Doubleday, 1924.

———. *A Personal Record*. Garden City, N.Y.: Doubleday, 1924.

———. *Tales of Unrest*. Garden City, N.Y.: Doubleday, 1920.

———. *'Twixt Land and Sea*. Garden City, N.Y.: Doubleday, 1924.

———. *Typhoon and Other Stories*. Garden City, N.Y.: Doubleday, 1920.

———. *Victory, An Island Tale*. Garden City, N.Y.: Doubleday, 1921.

Joyce, James. *The Critical Writings of James Joyce*. Edited by Ellsworth Mason and Richard Ellman. New York: Viking Press, 1959.

———. *Exiles*. New York: Viking Press, 1965.

———. *Finnegans Wake*. New York: Viking Press, 1971.

———. *A Shorter Finnegans Wake*. Edited by Anthony Burgess. New York: Viking Press, 1968.

———. *Letters of James Joyce*. Edited by Stua t Gilbert. 3 vols. New York: Viking Press, 1957.

———. *A Portrait of the Artist as a Young Man*. New York: Viking Press, 1967.

———. *Ulysses*. New York: Modern Library, 1961.

Forster, E. M. *Aspects of the Novel*. New York: Harcourt, Brace & World, 1954.

———. *The Collected Tales of E. M. Forster*. New York: Alfred A. Knopf, 1959.

———. *Howards End*. New York: Vintage Books, 1921.

———. *The Longest Journey*. New York: Vintage Books, 1962.

———. *Maurice*. New York: W. W. Norton & Co., 1971.

———. *A Passage to India*. New York: Harcourt, Brace and World, 1952.

———. *A Room with a View*. New York: Vintage Books, n.d.

———. *Two Cheers for Democracy*. New York: Harvest Books, 1951.

———. *Where Angels Fear to Tread*. New York: Vintage Books, 1920.

Lawrence, D. H. *The Collected Letters of D. H. Lawrence*. Edited by Harry T. Moore. 2 vols. London: Heinemann, 1962.

———. *The Complete Short Stories*. 3 vols. New York: Viking Press, 1967.

———. *D. H. Lawrence: Selected Literary Criticism*. Edited by Anthony Beal. New York: Viking Press, 1932.

———. *Lawrence in Love: Letters to Louie Burrows*. Edited by James T. Boulton. Nottingham: University of Nottingham Press, 1968.

———. *Sex, Literature, and Censorship*. Edited by Harry T. Moore. New York: Viking Press, 1953.

———. *The Trespasser*. London: William Heinemann, 1912.

———. *Women in Love*. New York: Viking Press, 1920.

Wagner, Richard. *Der Fliegende Holländer*. Complete Orchestral Score. London: Eulenburg, n.d.

———. *Der Fliegende Holländer*. Piano and Vocal Score. New York: G. Schirmer, 1897.

———. *Die Götterdämmerung*. Piano and Vocal Score. New York: G. Schirmer, n.d.

———. *My Life*. "Authorized Translation from the German." New York: Dodd, Mead & Co., 1911.

———. *Parsifal*. Complete Orchestral Score. London: Eulenburg, n.d.

———. *Parsifal*. Piano and Vocal Score. New York: G. Schirmer, 1904.

———. *Siegfried*. Piano and Vocal Score. Leipzig: Breitkopf and Härtel, 1914.

———. *Tristan und Isolde*. Piano and Vocal Score. New York: G. Schirmer, 1934.

———. *Wagner's Prose Works*. 8 vols. Translated by William Ashton Ellis. New York: Broude Brothers, 1966.

———. *Die Walküre*. Piano and Vocal Score. New York: G. Schirmer, 1904.

Woolf, Virginia. "Impressions at Bayreuth," ed. John L. Di Gaetani, *Opera News* 41 (August 1976): 22-23.

———. *Jacob's Room*. New York: Harcourt, Brace & World, 1959.

———. *The Voyage Out*. New York: Harcourt, Brace & World, 1948.

———. *The Waves*. New York: Harcourt, Brace & World, 1959.

———. *A Writer's Diary*. Edited by Leonard Woolf. New York: New American Library, 1953.

———. *The Years*. New York: Harcourt, Brace & World, 1965.

———, and Strachey, Lytton. *Letters*. Edited by Leonard Woolf and James Strachey. New York: Harcourt, Brace, and Co., 1956.

**Secondary Sources**

Aldington, Richard. *D. H. Lawrence: Portrait of a Genius But . . .* New York: Collier Books, 1950.

Annan, Noel Gilroy. *Leslie Stephen: His Thought and Character in Relation to his Time*. London: Macgibbon and Kee, 1951.

Arnold, Armin. "D. H. Lawrence, The Russians, and Giovanni Verga," *Comparative Literature Studies* 2 (1965): 249-57.

Auden, W. H. "James Joyce and Richard Wagner," *Common Sense* 10 (March 1941): 89-90.

Baine, Jocelyn. *Joseph Conrad: A Critical Biography*. New York: McGraw-Hill, 1959.

Barzun, Jacques. *Darwin, Marx, Wagner—Critique of a Heritage*. Boston: Little, Brown, & Co., 1941.

Beer, J. B. *The Achievement of E. M. Forster*. London: Chatto and Windus, 1962.

Bell, Quentin. *Bloomsbury*. London: Weidenfeld and Nicolson, 1968.

———. *Virginia Woolf, A Biography*. New York: Harcourt, Brace & Jovanovich, 1972.

Bennett, Arnold. *The Journal of Arnold Bennett*. New York: Literary Guild, 1933.

———. *Sacred and Profane Love*. London: Chatto and Windus, 1922.

Bennett, Joan. *Virginia Woolf: Her Art as a Novelist*. Cambridge: Cambridge University Press, 1949.

Bentley, Eric Russell. *A Century of Hero-Worship*. New York: J. B. Lippincott Co., 1944.

———. *The Cult of the Superman*. London: Robert Hale Ltd., 1947.

Blackstone, Bernard. *Virginia Woolf, A Commentary*. London: Hogarth Press, 1949.

Blissett, William F. "George Moore and Literary Wagnerism," *Comparative Literature* 13 (Winter 1961): 52-71.

———. "D. H. Lawrence, D'Annunzio, Wagner," *Wisconsin Studies in Contemporary Literature* 7 (1966): 21-46.

———. "Wagnerian Fiction in English," *Criticism* 5 (Summer 1963): 239-60.

Blunt, Wilfrid. *The Dream King: Ludwig II of Bavaria*. London: Hamish Hamilton, 1970.

Borrello, Alfred. *An E. M. Forster Glossary*. Metuchen, N.J.: The Scarecrow Press, 1972.

Bowen, Zack. "The Bronzegold Sirensong: A Musical Analysis of the Sirens Episode in Joyce's *Ulysses*." In *Literary Monographs*, edited by Eric Rothstein and Thomas K. Dunseath. Madison: University of Wisconsin Press, 1967.

Brewster, Dorothy. *Virginia Woolf*. New York: New York University Press, 1962.

Britten, Benjamin. "Some Notes on E. M. Forster and Music" in Oliver Stallybrass, ed., *Aspects of E. M. Forster*. New York: Harcourt, 1969.

Brown, Malcolm. *George Moore: A Reconsideration*. Seattle: University of Washington Press, 1955.

Budgen, Frank. *James Joyce and the Making of Ulysses*. Bloomington: Indiana University Press, 1960.

Burgess, Anthony. *Re-Joyce*. New York: Norton, 1965.

Campbell, Joseph, and Robinson, Henry Morton. *A Skeleton Key to Finnegans Wake*. New York: Harcourt, 1944.

Cavitch, David. *D. H. Lawrence and the New World*. New York: Oxford University Press, 1969.

Chastaing, Maxime. *La Philosophie de Virginia Woolf*. Paris: Presses Universitaires de France, 1951.

Coeuroy, André. *Wagner et l'Esprit Romantique*. Paris: Éditions Gallimard, 1965.

Conrad, Jessie. *Joseph Conrad and his Circle*. Port Washington, N.Y.: Kennikat Press, 1964.

Corke, Helen. *D. H. Lawrence: The Croyden Years*. Austin: University of Texas Press, 1965.

———. *Lawrence and Apocalypse*. New York: Haskell House, 1966.

Cowley, Malcolm, ed. *Writers at Work: The Paris Review Interviews*. New York: The Viking Press, 1957.

Daiches, David. *Virginia Woolf*. New York: New Directions, 1942.

D'Annunzio, Gabriele. *The Triumph of Death*. Translated from the Italian by Georgina Harding. London: William Heinemann, 1898.

———. *The Flame of Life*. Translated from the Italian by Baron Gustavo Tosti. New York: P. F. Collier and Son, 1970.

Delavenay, Emile. *D. H. Lawrence: The Man and his Work*. Translated from the French by Katharine Delavenay. London: Heinemann, 1972.

DeMichelis, Eurialo. *Tutto D'Annunzio*. Milan: Feltrinelli, 1960.

Donington, Robert. *Wagner's 'Ring' and Its Symbols: The Music and the Myth*. London: Faber and Faber, 1963.

Draper, Ronald P. *D. H. Lawrence*. New York: Twayne Publishers, 1964.

Dujardin, Édouard. *Le Monologue Intérieur: Son Apparition, Ses Origines, Sa Place dans l'Oeuvre de James Joyce*. Paris: Messein, 1931.

Eliot, T. S. *Poems, 1909-1925*. New York: Harcourt, 1925.

Ellmann, Richard. *James Joyce*. New York: Oxford University Press, 1959.

Epstein, Edmund L. *The Ordeal of Stephen Dedalus: The Conflict of the Generations in James Joyce's A Portrait of the Artist as a Young Man*. Carbondale: Southern Illinois University Press, 1971.

Fergusson, Francis. *The Idea of a Theatre*. Garden City, N.Y.: Doubleday, 1949.

Foerster-Nietzsche, Elizabeth, ed. *The Nietzsche-Wagner Correspondence*. With an Introduction by H. L. Mencken. Translated from the German by Caroline V. Kerr. New York: Liveright, 1921.

Ford, Ford Madox. *Joseph Conrad: A Personal Remembrance*. Boston: Little, Brown & Co., 1924.

Ford, George H. *Double Measure—A Study of the Novels and Stories of D. H. Lawrence*. New York: Holt, Rinehart, & Winston, 1965.

Forster, E. M. *Virginia Woolf*. New York: Harcourt, Brace, & Co., 1942.

Freeman, Mary. *D. H. Lawrence: A Basic Study of His Ideas*. New York: Grossett & Dunlop, 1955.

Galsworthy, John. *Letters from John Galsworthy, 1900-1932*. Edited by Edward Garnett. New York: Charles Scribner's Sons, 1934.

Gatch, Katharine A. "Conrad's Axel," *Studies in Philology* 48 (January 1951): 98-106.

Gilbert, Stuart. *James Joyce's Ulysses*. New York: Vintage Books, 1930.

Gillès, Daniel. *D. H. Lawrence ou Le Puritain Scandaleux*. Paris: René Julliard, 1964.

Gilman, Lawrence. *Wagner's Operas*. New York: Farrar & Rinehart, Inc., 1937.

Glasheen, Adaline. *A Second Census of Finnegans Wake: An Index of the Characters and their Roles*. Evanston: Northwestern University Press, 1963.

Gordon, John Dozier. *Joseph Conrad: The Making of a Novelist*. New York: Russell & Russell, 1963.

Gray, Ronald. *The German Tradition in Literature, 1871-1945*. Cambridge: Cambridge University Press, 1965.

Guiguet, Jean. *Virginia Woolf and her Works*. Translated from the French by Jean Stewart. London: Hogarth Press, 1962.

Gurko, Leo. "*The Trespasser*, D. H. Lawrence's Neglected Novel," *College English* 24 (October 1962): 29-35.

Gutman, Robert W. *Richard Wagner: The Man, His Mind, and His Music*. New York: Time Press, 1968.

Hall, Vernon, Jr. "Joyce's Use of Da Ponte and Mozart's *Don Giovanni*," *Publications of the Modern Language Association* 66 (March 1951): 78-84.

Hart, Clive. *Structure and Motif in Finnegans Wake*. Evanston: Northwestern University Press, 1962.

Haugh, Robert F. "Conrad's *Chance: Progression d'Effet*," *Modern Fiction Studies* 1 (February 1955): 9-15.

Hayman, David. "Tristan and Isolde in *Finnegans Wake:* A Study of the Sources and Evolution of a Theme," *Comparative Literature Studies* 1 (1964): 93-112.

Hinz, Evelyn J. "*The Trespasser:* Lawrence's Wagnerian Tragedy and Divine Comedy," *D. H. Lawrence Review* 4 (Summer 1971): 122-41.

Hochman, Baruch. *Another Ego: The Changing View of Self and Society in the Works of D. H. Lawrence*. Columbia: University of South Carolina Press, 1970.

Hodgart, Matthew, and Worthington, Mabel. *Song in the Works of James Joyce*. New York: Columbia University Press, 1959.

Hoffman, Frederick, J. *Freudianism and the Literary Mind*. Baton Rouge: Louisiana State University Press, 1957.

Hough, Graham. *The Dark Sun: A Study of D. H. Lawrence*. London: Duckworth, 1956.

Howarth, Herbert. *The Irish Writers, 1880-1940*. New York: Hill and Wang, 1958.

Hueffer, Francis. *Half a Century of Music in England, 1837-1887: Essays Toward a History*. London: Chapman and Hall, 1889.

———. *Richard Wagner*. London: Sampson Low, Marston, Searle, & Rivington, 1881.

Hynes, Samuel. *The Edwardian Turn of Mind*. Princeton, N.J.: Princeton University Press, 1968.

James, Henry. *Hawthorne*. New York: Harper and Row, 1879.

Jean-Aubry, Gérard. *The Sea Dreamer: A Definitive Biography of Joseph Conrad*. Translated from the French by Helen Sebba. Garden City, N.Y.: Doubleday, Page, & Co., 1957.

Johnstone, J. K. *The Bloomsbury Group: A Study of E. M. Forster, Lytton Strachey, Virginia Woolf, and their Circle*. New York: Farrar, Straus & Co., 1954.

Kain, Richard M. *Fabulous Voyager, A Study of James Joyce's Ulysses*. New York: Viking Press, 1947.

Karl, Frederick. *A Reader's Guide to Joseph Conrad*. New York: Noonday Press, 1960.

Kerman, Joseph. *Opera as Drama*. New York: Vintage Books, 1952.

Leavis, F. R. *The Great Tradition*. New York: New York University Press, 1967.

Litz, A. Walton. *The Art of James Joyce: Method and Design in Ulysses and Finnegans Wake*. London: Oxford University Press, 1961.

Loewenberg, Alfred. *Annals of Opera: 1597-1940*. Cambridge: W. Heffer & Sons, 1943.

Love, Jean O. *World in Consciousness: Mythopoetic Thought in the Novels of Virginia Woolf*. Berkeley: University of California Press, 1970.

Lynskey, Winifred. "The Role of the Silver in *Nostromo*," *Modern Fiction Studies* 1 (February 1955): 16-21.

MacCarthy, Desmond. *Leslie Stephen*. Cambridge: Cambridge University Press, 1937.

Magee, Bryan. *Aspects of Wagner*. New York: Stein and Day, 1968.

Maitland, Frederic William. *The Life and Letters of Leslie Stephen*. New York: G. P. Gutnam's Sons, 1906.

Mann, Thomas. *Essays of Three Decades*. Translated from the German by H. T. Lowe-Porter. New York: Knopf, 1947.

Marder, Herbert. *Feminism and Art, A Study of Virginia Woolf*. Chicago: University of Chicago Press, 1968.

Meyer, Bernard C. *Joseph Conrad: A Psychoanalytic Biography*. Princeton, N.J.: Princeton University Press, 1967.

Miko, Stephen J. *Toward Women in Love: The Emergence of a Lawrentian Aesthetic*. New Haven, Conn.: Yale University Press, 1971.

Mizener, Arthur. *The Saddest Story: A Biography of Ford Madox Ford*. New York: World Publishers, Inc., 1971.

Moore, George. *Confessions of a Young Man*. New York: Boni & Liveright, 1917.

———. *Evelyn Innes*. London: T. Fisher Unwin, 1898.

———. *Héloïse and Abélard*. New York: Boni and Liveright, 1921.

———. *Sister Teresa*. London: T. Fisher Unwin, 1901.

Moore, Harry T. *D. H. Lawrence: His Life and Work*. New York: Twayne Publishers, 1951.

———. *The Intelligent Heart: The Story of D. H. Lawrence*. New York: Grove Press, 1954.

Moser, Max. *Richard Wagner in der Englischen Literatur des XIX Jahrhunderts*. In *Schweizer Anglistische Arbeiten*. Bern: Verlag A. Francke, 1938.

Moynahan, Julian. *The Deed of Life, The Novels and Tales of D. H. Lawrence*. Princeton, N.J.: Princeton University Press, 1963.

Murry, J. Middleton. *Son of Woman*. London: Jonathan Cape, 1931.

Naremore, James. *The World Without a Self: Virginia Woolf and the Novel*. New Haven, Conn.: Yale University Press, 1973.

Nehls, Edward, ed. *D. H. Lawrence: A Composite Biography*. Madison: University of Wisconsin Press, 1957.

Newman, Ernest. *The Life of Richard Wagner*. 4 vols. New York: Alfred A. Knopf, 1933-1946.

Newman, Ernest. *Wagner as Man and Artist*. New York Vintage Books, 1924.

———. *The Wagner Operas*. New York: Alfred A. Knopf, 1963.

———. *A Study of Wagner*. New York: G. P. Putnam's Sons, 1899.

Nietzsche, Friedrich. *The Case of Wagner*. (No translator listed.) New York: Macmillan & Co., 1896.

Owens, Graham, ed. *George Moore's Mind and Art*. Edinburgh: Oliver and Boyd, 1968.

Pace, Billy James. "D. H. Lawrence's Use in his Novels of Germanic and Celtic Myth from the Music Dramas of Richard Wagner." Ph.D. dissertation, University of Arkansas, 1973.

Pound, Ezra. *The Letters of Ezra Pound to James Joyce*. Edited by Forrest Read. New York: New Directions, 1965.

Pritchard, R. E. *D. H. Lawrence: Body of Darkness*. London: Hutchinson University Library, 1971.

Reichelt, Kurt. *Richard Wagner und die Englische Literatur*. Leipzig: Xenien-Verlag, 1911.

Richter, Harvena. *Virginia Woolf: The Inward Voyage*. Princeton, N.J.: Princeton University Press, 1970.

Roberts, Warren. *A Bibliography of D. H. Lawrence*. London: Rupert Hart-David, 1963.

Sagar, Keith M. *The Art of D. H. Lawrence*. Cambridge: Cambridge University Press, 1966.

Said, Edward W. *Joseph Conrad and the Fiction of Autobiography*. Cambridge, Mass.: Harvard University Press, 1966.

Sharpe, Michael C. "The Genesis of D. H. Lawrence's *The Trespasser*," *Essays in Criticism* 11 (1961): 34-39.

Shaw, Bernard. *The Perfect Wagnerite*. London: Constable and Co., 1898.

Sherry, Norman. *Conrad's Eastern World*. Cambridge: Cambridge University Press, 1966.

Smith, James Penny. "Musical Allusions in James Joyce's *Ulysses*," Ph.D. dissertation, University of North Carolina, 1968.

Solomon, Margaret C. *Eternal Geomater: The Sexual Universe of Finnegans Wake*. Carbondale: Southern Illinois University Press, 1969.

Spilka, Mark. *The Love Ethic of D. H. Lawrence*. Bloomington: Indiana University Press, 1955.

Staley, Thomas F. *James Joyce Today, Essays on the Major Works*. Bloomington: Indiana University Press, 1966.

Stavrou, Constantine. "D. H. Lawrence's 'Psychology' of Sex," *Literature and Psychology* 6 (August 1956): 90-95.

Stein, Jack Madison. *Richard Wagner and the Synthesis of the Arts*. Detroit, Mich.: Wayne State University Press, 1960.

Stephen, Leslie. *History of English Thought in the Eighteenth Century*. 2 vols. New York: Harcourt, 1876.

Stoll, John E. *The Novels of D. H. Lawrence: A Search for Integration*. Columbia: University of Missouri Press, 1971.

Stone, Wilfrid. *The Cave and the Mountain, A Study of E. M. Forster*. Stanford, Calif.: Stanford University Press, 1966.

Strachey, Lytton. *Eminent Victorians*. New York: Harcourt, 1918.

Strong, L. A. G. "James Joyce and Vocal Music." In *Essays and Studies*, edited by V. de S. Pinto. Oxford: Clarendon Press, 1946.

Sultan, Stanley. "The Sirens at the Ormond Bar: *Ulysses*," *University of Kansas City Review* 26 (Winter 1959): 83-92.

Tedlock, E. W., Jr. *D. H. Lawrence, Artist and Rebel: A Study of Lawrence's Fiction*. Albuquerque: University of New Mexico Press, 1963.

Teets, Bruce E., and Gerber, Helmut E. *Joseph Conrad: An Annotated Bibliography of Writings about Him*. Dekalb: Northern Illinois University Press, 1971.

Thakur, N. C. *The Symbolism of Virginia Woolf*. London: Oxford University Press, 1965.

Thornton, Weldon. *Allusions in Ulysses*. Chapel Hill: University of North Carolina Press, 1961.

Tillyard, E. M. W. *The Epic Strain in the English Novel*. Fair Lawn, N.J.: Essential Books, 1958.

Tindall, William York. *A Reader's Guide to Finnegans Wake*. New York: Farrar, Straus and Giroux, 1969.

———. *A Reader's Guide to James Joyce*. New York: Noonday Press, 1959.

Villiers de l'Isle-Adam, Philippe Auguste. *Axël*. Translated from the French by June Guicharnaud. Englewood Cliffs, N.J.: Prentice-Hall, 1970.

Weston, Jessie. *The Legends of the Wagner Drama*. London: David Nutt, 1900.

———. *From Ritual to Romance*. Garden City, N.Y.: Doubleday, 1920.

Weininger, Otto. *Geschlect und Charakter*. Vienna: Wilhelm Braumüller, 1917.

Widmer, Kingsley. *The Art of Perversity: D. H. Lawrence's Shorter Fiction*. Seattle: University of Washington Press, 1962.

———. "The Primitive Aesthetic: D. H. Lawrence," *Journal of Aesthetics and Art Criticism* 17 (March 1959): 344-53.

Wilde, Oscar. *The Picture of Dorian Gray*. London: Ward, Lock & Bouden, 1895.

Wilde, Alan. *Art and Order: A Study of E. M. Forster*. New York: New York University Press, 1964.

Wiley, Paul L. *Conrad's Measure of Man*. New York: Gordian Press, 1954.

———. *Novelist of Three Worlds: Ford Madox Ford*. Syracuse, N.Y.: Syracuse University Press, 1962.

Wilson, Edmund. *Axel's Castle: A Study of the Imaginative Literature of 1870-1930*. New York: Charles Scribner's Sons, 1931.

———. *The Wound and the Bow, Seven Studies in Literature*. New York: Oxford University Press, 1929.

Woolf, Leonard. *Sowing: An Autobiography of the Years 1880 to 1904*. New York: Harcourt, Brace & Co., 1960.

———. *Growing: An Autobiography of the Years 1904-1911*. New York: Harcourt, Brace & Co., 1961.

———. *Beginning Again: An Autobiography of the Years 1911 to 1918*. New York: Harcourt, Brace & World, 1963.

———. *Downhill All the Way: An Autobiography of the Years 1919 to 1939*. New York: Harcourt, Brace & World, 1967.

———. *The Journey Not the Arrival Matters: An Autobiography of the Years 1939 to 1969*. New York: Harcourt, Brace & World, 1969.

Wyzewska, Isabelle. *La Revue Wagnérienne, Essai sur L'Interprétation Esthétique de Wagner en France*. Paris: Librairie Académique Perrin, 1934.

Yelton, Donald C. *Mimesis and Metaphor: An Inquiry into the Genesis and Scope of Conrad's Symbolic Imagery*. The Hague: Mouton, 1967.

Zuckerman, Elliott. *The First Hundred Years of Wagner's Tristan*. New York: Columbia University Press, 1964.

# Index